Sweet Water

Caitlin Press Inc.
8100 Alderwood Road,
Halfmoon Bay, BC V0N 1Y1
www.caitlin-press.com

Text design by Vici Johnstone
Cover art and design by Sharon Montgomery, cover layout by Vici Johnstone
Printed in Canada

Caitlin Press Inc. acknowledges financial support from the Government of Canada and the Canada Council for the Arts, and the Province of British Columbia through the British Columbia Arts Council and the Book Publisher's Tax Credit.

Library and Archives Canada Cataloguing in Publication
Sweet water : poems for the watersheds / edited by Yvonne Blomer.
Canadiana 20190173106 | ISBN 9781773860220 (softcover)
LCSH: Water—Poetry. | LCSH: English poetry—21st century.
LCC PN6110.W3 S94 2020 | DDC 821.008/036—dc23

# SWEET WATER

## Poems for the Watersheds

### EDITED BY
# YVONNE BLOMER

CAITLIN PRESS

for the waterways, small and large, buried and daylit, rushing and still,
may you flourish

for Colwyn
for the smallest rough-skinned newt, for those who fight for water

# Contents

watershed describes an area of land that contains a common set of streams and rivers that all drain into a single larger body of water, such as a larger river, a lake, or an ocean. In Canada, the Mackenzie River is the largest river flowing into the Arctic Watershed while the Fraser River is the largest river flowing into the Pacific Ocean watershed.

Have you also learned that secret from the river; that there is no such thing as time? That the river is everywhere at the same time, at the source and at the mouth, at the water-fall, at the ferry, at the current, in the ocean and in the mountains, everywhere and that the present only exists for it, not the shadow of the past nor the shadow of the future.
—**Hermann Hesse**, *Siddhartha*

# Driving Through: City, Forest, Watershed

Yvonne Blomer

Early October: I take a ferry from Victoria to Tsawwassen and drive east from the Pacific Ocean to the Fraser River, through the Fraser Valley, along the Chilliwack River to the Skagit River and on through rolling hills to Vernon. The highway follows the rivers and their industries—boat building, logging, fishing—through small towns and growing cities. I notice trees felled and trees growing up from the banks of the rivers and lakes, some dying, some dead, some burnt in recent fires while others stand majestic on the cusp of autumn. A truck passes with a massive section of pipe on its back and I wonder if it will be for water or for the unwanted pipeline, as I do not have the knowledge to discern pipes. I move through the richly intertwined landscape of the coastal and inland watersheds of British Columbia. Later, as I drive north through Lillooet, snow comes down the mountain and lightly blankets bright red and auburn trees in a patch above a river. Overcome by the beauty of it, I burst into tears. Here I am, on a road solely for humans, cutting through the landscape of the wild earth in my carbon-emitting car. I pass a clean-up crew at a mudslide near Lillooet and wonder how the entire mountain hasn't come sliding down. We are imperilled humans on a fragile planet. I drive—enthralled by riveting drop-offs to the right, my eyes dangerously drawn there.

I want this road so I can coast through such spaces and lay my eyes on each nook and cranny, stand at a river, breathe autumn's offering, put my hand in the water, drink from it. But I want the road gone so that these spaces can exist plastic- and toxin-free, with only the bear's droppings, the deer's footprint. I see a plastic bag caught on a rock and I do not flinch. I flinch. I keep my eyes to the road, rumble of my new snow tires and my alertness keeping me on this damnable glorious road.

We are the watersheds. From birth to death our bodies are water and waste. Our reliance on water is pure and unrelenting. Rather than covet and protect water and the species, plants, insects, and birds that rely on it, we place ourselves above all things and are poor stewards for this planet.

Globally, much has changed since *Refugium: Poems for the Pacific* came out in the fall of 2017. Scientists, under the Liberal government, began to speak out and be heard again. Young activists, too, are speaking and being heard. Poets, too, are writing more and more of ecological loss and grief. The US, however, under the Trump administration, intends to withdraw from the Paris Climate Agreement and, according *The New York Times*, has put in place rollbacks that will increase greenhouse gasses and lead to thousands of deaths from poor air and water quality. While *Refugium* may have been just ahead of its time, *Sweet Water* arrives mid-stream. It adds a diverse and critical range of voices to the chorus of youths, scientists, students, and city municipalities who are speaking for water. Poets here articulate connections to water and long-held concerns for it. They have been paying attention to varied and loved watery places, water systems, ecologies, and vanishing creatures.

Simone Weil writes in *Gravity and Grace*, "The poet produces the beautiful by fixing attention on something real." This close attention and the resulting poems in *Sweet Water* remind us of our connection to water and our complicated dependence on it. We are reminded, too, of the profound grief we feel for our part in damaging the natural ecosystems of the planet. Here the poets say: Listen. And now is the time for listening, for deeply contemplating the planet, her watersheds and the creatures who rely on them. It is a time for profound change.

Notes and Readings:
Simone Weil, *Gravity and Grace*, trans. Emma Crawford and Mario von der Ruhr, (New York: Routledge Classics, New York, reprint, 2004), 119.

# The Body of Water and Its Spirit

**Philip Kevin Paul**

...imagine that even a puddle of water is a living thing, and it has a life, a spirit, and spiritedness.

Some years back, I took a job with the Institute of Ocean Sciences (IOS). My job was to compare and correlate traditional W̱SÁNEĆ knowledge with current scientific "discovery." In the earliest meetings, the department heads and upper echelon of the IOS attended. They took the lead in explaining that, essentially, the water in Brentwood Bay, W̱SÁNEĆ people's front yard on the west side of the Saanich Peninsula, doesn't move. This means the water in the bay doesn't flush out or cleanse itself in the same way as other bays and most bodies of water. After explaining this, they asked if my people had a name for this body of water. I answered, SX̱OX̱IYEM, which means "still water." They had been studying the bay for thirty-plus years. This was a doorway between two ways of knowing.

In another meeting soon after, I met with a more intimate crowd, the staff and heads of departments I would be reporting to directly. They asked me, when I thought of the project, was there anything that came to mind immediately. I responded, "Yes, ḴENNES, the stream that runs below our graveyard and has been an essential stream for our people prior to settler contact." The silence that followed this proclamation was mystery-filled for me. Eventually their answer to me was, "That's freshwater. We are *ocean* scientists." They weren't dismissing the relationship between fresh and saltwater, they just hadn't expected this answer out of me. My people's territory is mostly ocean, and the scientists wanted, more than anything, my people's understanding of the ocean.

In time, the scientists taught me about how rain saturates ground, and that the water that isn't absorbed is called runoff, and it goes wherever it ends up. Our streams rely on this pattern or system. They also taught me that while water saturation maintains a freshwater table through this process, the maintenance of that freshwater table also keeps the ocean from its desire to rise up from underground. They also explained that roads, houses and parking lots, for instance, interrupt the even maintenance of the freshwater tables.

In W̱SÁNEĆ our most sacred tree is called ḰOḰOIȽĆ, which refers to the Arbutus tree; it means "water drinking tree." It holds water, and drinks it sparingly, so when there is a drought, it endures better than other trees.

One of the most beautiful things I encountered in my entire life was when I was at the Institute of Ocean Sciences. They were surprised, but not baffled, that my first request, when working at the IOS, was that I wanted to talk about a freshwater stream. At first, I wondered if I was being taken seriously, then they rented a helicopter and hired a videographer, and we went up after a big rain. From the air, there was a very clear *plume* between the saltwater and the freshwater. As I looked down, I was reminded that fresh water is no longer drinkable in W̱SÁNEĆ and that two of our essential streams have disappeared because they have been diverted into ditches.

In the entire world, there aren't many waterfalls that land directly into the ocean, but there are two right here in W̱SÁNEĆ and in SX̱OX̱IYEM. Here in W̱SÁNEĆ, the one called K̓ENNES is where a whale beached itself, and the other, called WEĆEĆE, is a particular sound in the W̱SÁNEĆ ear, and it is the song of the stream. Really, they are beacons, sending out a signal that attracts little beings like insects, and the insects attract tiny fish who go there to feed, and the fish attract bigger and bigger fish until the salmon come, and then the whales come to eat the salmon.

Our bay was where whales used to calf. It was a time of peace between all whales. The bulls didn't come into the bay unless there was need for them. When I was very young, my grandpa took me to the beach near K̓ENNES, and he said that once, at the entrance to the bay, he saw that a female was in distress, and two bulls turned and came to the female's aid. A calf was having trouble rising, half in its birth sac, so the bulls put the calf on their backs and dove and came up, dove and came up, until the calf was swimming on its own. He said we had a song for that occasion, and he sang that song for me, then he lay in my lap and cried. I don't know how old he was, but I was five or six, and it was the first time I saw an adult cry. "This song isn't sung anymore," he said, "because the whales aren't here anymore." And then he sang me a song.

Remember, water is a living thing to W̱SÁNEĆ people and it has a spirit, and with its particular spiritedness, because it has its own shape, the spirit of water might lie with you in your sleep because you visited it that day. It wants you to understand that your desires are more fluid than we are often willing to accept. Our dreams that night, when the spirit of water is with us, are of acceptance, despite how we understand beauty and honour, and we are touched for a time, and held in the shape that we might truly accept, for once, ourselves.

# Water

**George Szirtes**

The hard beautiful rules of water are these:
That it shall rise with displacement as a man
does not, nor his family. That it shall have no plan
or subterfuge. That in the cold, it shall freeze;
in the heat, turn to steam. That it shall carry disease
and bright brilliant fish in river and ocean.
That it shall roar or meander through metropolitan
districts whilst reflecting skies, buildings and trees.

And it shall clean and refresh us even as we slave
over stone tubs or cower in a shelter or run
into the arms of a loved one in some desperate quarter
where the rats too are running. That it shall have
dominion. That it shall arch its back in the sun
only according to the hard rules of water.

old engravings
on a tarnished silver tray—
late winter lake

**Art Fredeen**,
Lake Ontario, February 2018

# I. Sweet

Sweet water
is any naturally occurring water except seawater and brackish water.
Sweet water includes water in ice sheets, ice caps, glaciers, ice-
bergs, bogs, ponds, lakes, rivers, streams, and even underground water
called groundwater. Sweet Water can easily become polluted by human activities
or due to naturally occurring processes, such as erosion.

My 'place of clear water', / the first hill in the world
where springs washed into / the shiny grass.
—**Seamus Heaney**

# AMNIOTIC

**Susan Stenson**

Inside your mother
the song of the song
of the watershed.
It cannot hold. Cannot think.
Cries for vengeance, not logic.

Out of water, the first word:
Drink. A woman wakes from another
nightmare and still finds herself
thinking: paradise, bliss.

There is no grief like water's.
One hand under the old pump
the long yellow years
the length of two cranes.

# THE WATER HEART

**Story Charlie Neyelle, form Thos Nesbitt**
*with permission of the Déline Elders*

The Elders of the Sahtugot'ine—
"The people belonging to Sahtu"—
Have passed down a story
Through many generations:

In times past, their spiritual teachers were often
"Mystically tied" to different parts of the world:
Some to the caribou,
Some the wolf,
Some the northern lights,
Some the willow.

Etsé Daoyé was one such person.
He lived all around Sahtu—
"Great Bear Lake" in the English language—
But made his home primarily in Edaiila
On the northeast shores of the Lake.

Etsé Daoyé was mystically tied to the loche.
One day, after setting four hooks, he found one of them missing.
This disturbed him:
In those days hooks were rare and very valuable.

That night he travelled
In his dreams
With the loche
In search of the fish that had
Taken his hook.

As he traveled through the
Centre of Sahtu
He became aware of a great
Power in the lake—
The heart of the lake
Which the Elders name the "Water Heart".

Etsé Daoyé contemplated this heart.
He became aware that it is
Connected to all beings—

The land,
The sky,
Plants,
Other creatures,
People—

It helps sustain the watershed of Sahtu, and
The rivers of the watershed are the veins of the
Organism that is the watershed.
Fish array themselves all round the water heart, and
The great peninsulas of the lake
Bow in respect to this heart.

The elders of the Sahtugot'ine stress the
The interconnectedness of all things
Sahtugot'ine and non-Sahtugot'ine alike.

From the universal law of the
Interconnectedness of things flows
Our responsibility to
Care for this world.
We do this by treating it and
All beings with
Utmost respect.

# PROVINCIAL LETTER

**Nicholas Bradley**

> *... the sky cleared as if the white sediment there had sunk ...*
> —Virginia Woolf, *The Waves*

And when at last the rains end, shadows flare
up and water chases water, the rivers

of rivers on Vancouver's sodden Island
inundating already flooded banks

although the glaring light at mid-morning
is frozen. The croaking bird is frozen too,

its branch iced over. Muscled rivers flex
and bulge; every other becomes another.

The far bay, where flattened, sliding current
runs its course, is *mezzo-forte*. Here the high

falls clamour rather rudely as the glum
crow opens his mouth soundlessly before

admitting brute defeat.
What intelligence dapples lank trees

on the northern shore and flickers on thin
crusts of snow above rapids? Is it

only the unembarrassed sun, or is
January's brilliant abstraction

an attestation that rivers, the bird
and its bough, inlet and tide all listen

to rivers and birds, to trees, to tides,
to falls, rock, light? As skies clear, as if white

sediment had sunk to the stream's
rumpled bed, the cold Puntledge and the cold

Tsolum ferry the debris of mountains
and forests to the strait, a belated

owl *who-who*ing. And home now I compose
a missive to my napping son that someday

I may finish. This afternoon it contains
crude instructions for spotting piney

finches as they melt into the canopy,
for knowing how little words say of rivers

and islands. The sublime lies all around,
as familiar as the tousled, trodden ground.

He sleeps; I write; we make no sound.

# ANTLER RIVER

**Laurie D. Graham**

Pigeon waltzing the trail on one foot and one little nub.
Mallards and their escaped domestic kin and the bright,
rasping horns of Canada geese in false spring, in glacier-
turquoise water. Hundreds and hundreds of sharps sinking
into the banks. Nests of clothes. Tents. Tarps. Broken trees
helped down the banks with chainsaws. Water rainbow-slicked.
The salt-spackled ground. The farmed transplants, the white-
bread crumbs. Up the bank: courthouse, hockey arena,
brutalist government tower, city museum, wind.

  Down here, the fork in the river. The sacred.

# SKEIN

**Kim Goldberg**

The river is a skein of silver geese
beating, turning, calling through a tangled
hymn. The shadows long, the forest raw
Eyes of coal among the limbs

Beating, turning, crawling through a tangled
room, we try to find a door
Eyes of coal among the limbs
A clock falls off the glossy wall

Your tomb we try to find—a door
to chambered pools where eggs are left
A rock falls off the mossy wall
Each salmon is a feathered scythe

in chambered pools where eggs are left
Now we lay us down to sleep
Each salmon is a feathered scythe
beneath our heads. Strange dreams do blaze

Now we lay us down to sleep
upon a gaping pit of tar
Beneath our heads strange dreams do blaze
with firestorms and wailing trees

Upon a gaping pit of tar
this hymn of shadows long, forest raw
with firestorms and wailing trees
The river was a skein of silver geese

# SMALL SONG FOR THE WATERSHEDS

**Iain Higgins**

*after Pierre de Ronsard, after pseudo-Anacreon*

Earth's waters quench its thirst,
  As trees drink deep in dirt;
The wide seas drink from streams,
  The sun drinks up the seas.

The moon too sips the sun.
  All things drink, both high and low,
Subject to a common law:
  So let's pour them a pure one!

# Dharana

**Barbara Black**

*Upper Lynn Valley, 1932*

*Varley knifes on impasto*
*Vera genuflects, behind her*
*Lynn Peak a purple breast*

The valley then was timber-stripped
rotten-teeth stumps, snags
stuck in soil
like dirty toothpicks
he paints
divinity colonizing the slash
It pains me with wonder, he says

*Upper Lynn Valley, 2010*

*viscous green on underlay of black*
*light sucked up by fir and hemlock*
*iron oxide seeps brown blood*

We hike there
long before the hordes arrive
Lynn Peak a pyramid
half-shadowed in sun
red-backed salamander
holds the mountain in its eye
Lynn Creek weeps water
through canyon walls
the old cedars watch us
make love by the pools
that drain to the inlet
where orcas slip ghostlike
through a salmonless sea

*cigarette to lips, he drags*
*his hand through his hair*
*iridescent sky sticks to one strand*

# A Brief History of Settlement on Hamilton Mountain, from 1789

**John Terpstra**

We came to a place
after many days walking,
the top of a cliff,
a plateau of wood and meadow,
and followed a creek
to its sweet water's source
below an outcrop of rock
tall enough to provide a broad view
of this oasis from the strife we had so recently suffered
in another land.
We gave thanks, and chose to stay,
as did all our company, each family
planting itself by spring and pond
of creeks whose paths they followed
from waterfalls over that long cliff
which served as a protective rampart to our community
for seven generations,
until the young city mounted its height,
stormed our fields and woodlots,
buried the creeks in pipes,
and sent springs into hiding
beneath the trees,
the few left standing—
                    the trees,
those intermediaries between ourselves
and our Maker,
whose roots never cease to divine
the living waters
that my people, naked
under shower heads, with kitchen faucets
running full blast,
                    forget.

# When the Rain Comes

**Russell Thornton**

When the rain comes, it is here to see us
and is here to see the bones of the dead in the earth of cemeteries
and the ashes of the dead scattered wherever they may be scattered.

*I will tell it, and tell it, and tell it, and tell it,*
I heard a voice say as I was waking from a dream of rain.

When the rain arrives, it is light falling,
cups of light beyond number falling, shattering, and becoming raindrops—
baby steps of water that lead light away and away.
*I will tell it, and tell it, and tell it, and tell it.*

When the rain comes, light falls and bathes
in its change, it cries out in a touch, and the rain lifts and is still
and is a conception as visible as all that is lit, and is a perfect surprise—
*I will tell it, and tell it, and tell it, and tell it.*

When the rain comes, it brings with it
the past of someone I loved and who is gone,
and when the rain comes, it opens arms broken and waiting—
the rain of these arms can never open the same way twice.

When the rain arrives, the burning light
that falls as rain and that turns us to ash
reveals to us that what we will become
is what we see around us, and it reveals this for the first time—
*I will tell it, and tell it, and tell it, and tell it.*

When the rain comes, when the touch of the rain arrives,
it is here to touch back to itself through us,
and is here to let us be its mirror, and what we show
is nothing but ourselves arriving at mirror after varying mirror—
*I will tell it, and tell it, and tell it, and tell it.*

When the rain comes, water looks back at the light
that brought it here to see us, the way I sometimes mistake
my fingers for another's hair, or my mouth for another's mouth of rain,
and that person vanishes into light, when the rain comes.

# WEATHER IN DUBLIN

## Rob Taylor

The night Heaney died it rained so hard in Vancouver the gutters clogged,
flooding the streets. In all our years in the city we'd never seen rain like it.
We shouted as much to our neighbours, who were all at their windows,
and they nodded and laughed and agreed. We went down to the street,
barefoot with umbrellas, and danced like Gene Kelly and Debbie Reynolds.

The night Heaney died an old woman two buildings down raced out in a rain slicker
boots and rubber gloves, and worked with a broom at the storm drains. She hauled up
leaves and feathers and plastic containers and—god knows how—a rock the size
of two fists. We stopped and watched as water rose up, breached the curb, rushed
over lawns and flower beds, sloshed against apartment blocks. Humiliated,
we stooped next to the woman and lowered our hands into the swirling dark.

The night Heaney died it was morning in Dublin, so what am I going on about?
It was thirteen degrees and partly cloudy. Visibility good, wind from the southwest.
The light that slanted in through the window was bright enough and soft, I imagine
like the light that greeted us this morning when we awoke and learned the news.

Below, our neighbours have made their way outside. They are gathering up
the scattered heads of flowers and talking to one another. One has a rake,
another a clear plastic bag. A third has a phone and is calling around
about water damage. Two are distributing paper cups full of coffee
and the rest are drinking from them. We will remember this morning forever,
I am almost sorry to say.

# CHILDHOOD: DANFORD LAKE

**Thos Nesbitt**

When I was younger, I slept
Through uncounted summer days,
In a log house by a lake,
And woke with the lapping of the waves,
The gentlest sound.
And sunlight and shadows
Reflected on the ceiling,
As voiceless as the northern lights,
And the first restless stirring of the wind,
And my mind the blue sky.
Awoke to the jays
In the soaring trees,
And the mist-strewn lake,
And the worn boards of the rowboat
On my feet,
And the creak of the oarlocks
In the still-quiet world.

The sun spirals down
In the depths of the water,
Green and gold
On ancient stones,
And logs left by
A distant time,
Unchanging now,
And fish pass by
Like dreams.

And I peered in the water
Days and days long,
As the sun arced 'cross the sky,
And the wash of the poplars' leaves
Bore me away,
With turtles lumbering
Far below.

And the wind rose and fell,
And the dusk came again,
With the sounds of the fire,
And the distant lights
Across the lake.
And I slept through whirring,
Star-filled nights,
In whippoorwills' raucous,
Liquid songs,
The far-away call of the loons,
And logs wrapped
All about me.

# I am the Sweet Water

**Raine Gutierrez**

I am the sweet water.
You are the osprey that panics all the fish in my body.

I am the glacier water.

You are the shy
solitary snow leopard
with keen eyes.

You are an endangered animal.
and my glacier is melting too quickly.

I am a lake.

You are the carbon dioxide changing my water
into a brew of carbonic acid.

Where did the sweet water go?

# ANIMAL TO WATER, 2005

**Ishtar**

On a sunny afternoon near the end of summer
I finally have an opportunity to swim in this lake.

From his truck tire inner-tube
he watches for my signal that I'm done,
ready to guide me back to the shore I can't see, can't find.

I lean forward at the cusp, then plunge.
Lifted, lulled, loosened,
I'm sliding like a dream through water's silky body,
a fast-moving stream of power, within the body of water's power.

The lake is peaceful. It holds its power softly.

Easy with grace, I extend my rolling spine and reach.
Precise, sleek, water fleet
I feel like I'm flying
finned

I forget my shell of yearning,
leave it without noticing
as I stroke myself through the thousand arms of water.

Away from the heavy hand of shore
I push my strength
work on evening my kick out.
Wash off the slimy remarks of that body builder
smoking and puffing himself up on the shady wedge of beach.

Sweet men, scary men
I sense them checking me out.
I want the sweet,
some kind of simple,
but not too simple,

transparent to twenty feet and then
something tremendous sleeping below.

Awaken!
Raft man, or the one who offered to be my swimming partner,
what else under the sun would you offer?

And Mr. Body Builder of the bulked-up ego and thin-skinned salamander underbelly,
you, like billions of others, are physically formidable;
I also came from the gym,
straight from doing weights to the lake
to stalk into the middle of
an unfamiliar crowd
as an animal woman
strong, ready.

Don't touch me with those beliefs or hands!
Let me swim. Let me be what I am!

I curve with the shoreline,
jewel the water with bubbles and fervour,
throwing in the truest things I have,
repetitions of breath
the flash of my hands
the way they pull me through
my continuing heart

In this water, freedom reigns,
air and heart for the underneath in me.

But now I'm fighting through clumps of tough, stringy green
that wraps around me like twine;
and masses of lily pads that suck at my hands,
take my breath in their palms
remind me I could drown,
be prey

Tangled in fear I tell myself to relax,
breathe slowly,
be soft like the water
trust how it holds me
Lay myself out and praise its generosity.
There is no abyss under me,
no monsters,
no claws of icy pain to tear the motion from my lungs.
This water has chosen to float me above.

The tongues of the water are warm and light.
It tastes of lake mud and greenness and paradise.

Lake swimming is a prayer and a push for survival
that broke out of a closed box world,
an unpackaging of my naked, curving ways
from the straight-line journey that tries to take me endlessly
back and forth across the grid-grind;
north, south, east, west
hard-closed corners
so many fences.

Swimming here with the unobtrusive aid I need
given only when I need it
frees a relationship between equals.

I take all my power
a hard exercise of my unbroken will
supported in the body of the vast beloved
a freed exaltation!

I hear the hissing crackle of my passage,
my thrilling body
a racing, white, electric stream
my flood water body
joining with and cleaving
the might of the lake
plowing through the water so fast now

I can no longer be tracked by sighted, human eyes
can leap invisible into another kind of time
leaving just these things:
indelible in their minds, the recognition of cageless ability
and written across the surface of the lake in sweat and hot flow,
this animal's love letter.

# THIS VOICE OF WATER

**Lauren Elle DeGaine**

*A response to W.S. Merwin's "After the Alphabets"*

I am trying to decipher the language of water
lapping a sigh that aches
liquid nouns churning in sandy mouths
dripping down sprawled stone breasts—
water speaks
utters the ages
foreshadowing
drop by drop
its voice a yawing drumbeat
a warning

# Parts Per Billion

**Joe Zucchiatti**

Someone must have figured
they were too good to throw away,
so for the past sixty years or so,
my family has stored
the cabin's drinking water
in two repurposed, galvanized steel pails
still bearing the stickers from their previous life:
SOLVIT: Professional Rat and Mouse Killer

"Well, those were rinsed out, believe me,"
my grandmother said
when my five-year-old son—
hyperlexic, early to read, at eye-level with the water pails—
finally noticed

so we continue to strain
the algae-thick lake water
through an old bedsheet
and into the pest control buckets,
somehow maintaining faith
that the decades-old fabric
is filtering out the algal blooms,
the creosote from the recycled, railroad tie dock,
the acid rain and the local paper mill effluent,
the petrol rainbows leaking from motorboats,
and the piss and shit of all god's creatures
in the nearby swamp

the living water,
my uncle proclaims proudly, defiantly,
as if purified water
was only for sissies,
and impurity and pollution
somehow nutritious

and it's true that no one's gotten seriously ill

but you can't help but wonder
every time your stomach gurgles

and you can't help but notice
that that side of the family's
pretty goddamned weird.

# Mountain Stream

**Lee Beavington**

the slither of trail disappears
whispers of mosquito
rise to my breath

seduced by cedar
I wind down the mountainside
pathless

at first a faint trickle
water sirens drum up
a thousand gravity spirits
awaken my numbed senses

river currents stretch
as umbilical cords
from cloud to expectant sea

I pause on the shore
whitecap thresholds
roar in a slender ravine
beyond the boulder
water limbs claw
at my synthetic shell

Who is this self
that I always meet here?

I am trapped
between rapids and cliff
virgin maidenhair fern
every crevice wet

I cannot tell
if this pulsating wall of rock
is my spine
or the water

my only path—
the algae-slick stones
my ankle twists
on a rock's fur
foot thrust
to earth's riverfloor

I reach for a stem
fifty spines needle my hand
the bite of devil's club
releases my blood
into the mountain's heart

the river tugs at my thighs
a place no civilized man
should steep in
ridged spruce
taller than the sun
I will all trails
to be washed away
in a moment
of animal surrender
I will my veins
to open
the way this forest
and all that is living here
opens in me

# Ubi Sunt

**M.W. Jaeggle**

Not closer to the words petrified by value,
but the wind's dry flowing,
the gossip exchanged between aster and
the lance-tip leaves exiled from the salal bush.
Appetite without measure or shadow,
the ground in August desires only clouds.
Snow nears, though—you can hear it,
you can hear it laugh where the clay cracks its lip
on the bone-edge of the trail.
What was the shrill of insipid grass, then,
but the penitent soil whispering,
repeat a word enough and it'll turn into water.

# The Weight of Snow

**Michelle Poirier Brown**

> *In some places, pebbles were as abundant as if we had been travelling upon the*
> *bed of some former river or lake; the mind endeavours in vain to establish limits*
> *to the vast expanse of water which certainly at some former day overflowed the*
> *whole of that country.* —W.H. Keating, 1823

We are the sodden soils left by the biblical flood—
when the Agassiz basin burst through the Laurentide Ice Sheet,
Noah set sail on the Black Sea.

It is snow I think of when I think of watershed.
Snow so deep, it kills you.

Snow so deep, bulldozers pile it into banks eight feet high both sides of the highway.
If you come around a corner to meet a metal wall, two dozers dos-à-dos,
you drive up.
The car slows, slides down sideways.

Snow. Frozen floodwater.
On a clear day, you can see months down the road.
Centimetres fallen counted against equipment costs.
Will it go suddenly? Will it rain when the creeks are full?

Snowmelt seeps through the bank into the river,
the sponge of land leaking under the weight of snow.
The ice on the river heaves, groans. You can tell by the sound
when it is time to go to the dock and watch.
You can hear it for blocks.

We watch to see if the bridge can take it,
if the steel-tipped concrete stanchions will stand.
If the ministry of bridges will set dynamite.

We live at the bottom of a lake, now extinct,
thumbprint of a glacier
whose comings and goings shaped the world.
Whose ghost rises every spring.

# Beautiful Boys

**Brian Brett**

The pretty ones, hard and lean
dashing into the gap through the trees,
hurling themselves at the river pool,
from branches, from rocks, from ropes—
naked to the clean water that beads
them with the dew of a river catching
light on young skin in sun and shadow,
me jostling at their side, not knowing
if I was beautiful, if I was wild,
if I was lost, or if I was just another boy.
It didn't matter then, not on that day;
spangled in the heat of summer,
peering into cataracts, the deep,
the terror that rushed between rocks
struck vermilion by the falling sun
while the bright scroll of our lives
lay unwritten before us like a river.
What counted was the run to the edge
and that scissored,
   leg-thrashing
      leap into ....

# Pitcher Plant

**Kurt Trzcinski**

Time measured in a different clock
the sun a different strength
the earth of another age

1.
A young plant pushes a new leaf
toward the falling light
guarded by jungle canopies
this leaf remains folded
deformed
collecting dew

2.
Humid air gathers in white clouds
mist forms into heavy dark layers
releasing rain with a rumble
that shakes the earth

Water drops
with one small grain of dust

the seed of clouds
returns

3.
Roots spread and reach
each finger pushes soil aside
seeking nutrients

Bacteria from the canopy above
explore the crevices of this new leaf
to find energy
then die

4.
Cells open to nourishment
life from a leaf
feed seeds

A channel opens

5.
An ant leaves the warm scent of her sisters
to search for food
slips on the smooth waxy leaf
struggles for life
surface tension breaks
and she gulps water
to the bottom

6.
A decomposing body breaks and disappears
the protist waves a flagella
directs a single cell to the mouth

7.
Sweet nectar strengthens a mosquito's wings
laden with eggs, she searches for water to place them
tests, smells for bacteria-food
drops her young

8.
Larvae flick and feed
collect, gather, and direct bacteria, ciliates and rotifers
to the mouth

Some brothers and sisters die,
descend to the bottom to decay
in the depths
of the pitcher plant

9.
A small fly from the river bottom
finds a new home for her offspring
they will struggle less than their ancestors
eating dead leaves and ants
in the deep protected home

10.
A large, tabanid fly
smells the meat of mosquito and midge
and lays her eggs
providing new hunting grounds for carnivores

channels open

11.
A spider reaches for her sticky string
draws cables together
now ready to trap
those that near the bubbling ecosystem
of the pitcher plant

12.
The tiny-lake, light and golden-green
teems with bacteria and algae
browns with decaying detritus
from the bottom
stirred by a scientist

Drops of water in a vial
angels of cilia and bacteria
quickly die
along with a hope to unlock secrets
Old channels close

13.
One leaf severed, placed in a zip-
lock bag and frozen
with death intact

14.
Colourful slides presented to a small academic audience
all admire the beauty and complexity of the micro-world
 —ponder—

What remains unknown


and open

# BLUEROOF

**Brent Raycroft**

We park in the little lot near Kim Ondaatje's house
just as three ATVs arrive with kids in bathing suits
and the mom of some of them, all helmetless, more local
than us I guess, and since they are a noisy bunch
we put some distance between us by setting out
upon the path that gives the public access to the acres at the back
purchased for safe keeping by the Land Conservancy:
a wooded elephantine rise of Canadian Shield.

We pass the cattle and familiar gate (we've been here before
visiting the artist), slow down among the giant maples,
reach the footbridge over Depot Creek with jokes of trolls,
but we're not dressed to go exploring those wet rocks, so we hike on
until we're at the brim of the beaver pond,
the still wide top of the watershed, where we stop
and consider what this place might have meant
to a painter or writer or settler or native inhabitant.

Returning we meet them again—at the bridge
where they're swimming or climbing or sitting in the stream.
They're not a crowd but a composition now,
each on a wet black stone with a different ability
and each of them staring at us as we talk
with the mom about places like this and their rarity
except for the one peering steadily into a pool at the edge
and the one with her arms thrust deep in the turbulence.

# WATER TO WATER

**Kate Braid**

*With thanks to Seamus Heaney for "Lightenings iv"*

Under the guardian cap of the water's surface
this swimmer finds another
memory, long-forgotten motion flowing

through arms, legs, twist of her body turning
as if some ancient instruction
bubbling through her, remembered at last

this is why the hairs on her arms, her head, grow
like this, why her nose so shields her breath, caress
of waves, diamond pattern of flickering light
beneath her.

Bare to her body's memory, how safe and right
it feels to be a new-born, fish, alive again,
the body's grace joined, thirst quenched,
water to water.

# Thirst

**Daniel Cowper**

In February, creeks are reduced to ice,
dry creek-beds and banks burst

with frost-jacks like unclipped claws.
One weekend I go looking for you

on a wooded hillside where underfoot
the slope-scree breaks and sinks. Here

hemlocks grow close,
choking each other for sky. I pull myself uphill

by their trunks, caking hands
with resin and grit. I recognize

your gully from last fall and remember
how, parched from climbing

I heard you clatter down this thin ravine,
came, filled my dirty palms with you and drank.

Now you're gone. Greenstone in the sikebed
rattles behind me as I climb to the wetland

at the creek's root. In autumn you pooled here
between huge cedars, tinkling like door-chimes

as rainwater dripped from the cedar scales above.
Now milky wheels of cat-ice lie flat

between the trees, curlicued where eels of air
writhed inside the airtight crust

as inch by inch you sank away.
You vanished into soil,

leaving fossils of your surface
over hollow cups of dirt.

# STONE'S DEEP ACCORD, ITS STEADY PRESENCE

**Wendy Donawa**

Snow on stone. Crystalized for seconds, for eons,
their specific gravities meet.
Snow smokes over elk pastures
sloping the blaze and splatter of late aspens
against the evergreen of lodgepole pine, of spruce
carpeting ancient inland seas
now draped above valleys.

Reefs
crenellated
dogtooth, lace, sawback
pouring scree down cross-hatched gullies
sending shale, sandstone, limestone
spilling this chert, cousin to flint, to chalcedony.
And slate, shale's bastard progeny, fine-grained,
foliated, its fossils' traces
measuring Earth's timescales.

Compressed for millennia
by time's upheavals; striations
sent thundering down the tilt
of layered shelves, oystered in glaciers,
cobbling waterways that loop the continent.
Erosion's runes inscribe its journey.

Stone's deep accord, its steady presence
woven into the world's fabric of being.
Now grounded, stone as witness, as clarification.
Starlight gathers stone with tranquility.
Sun traces it with shadow.
Rain's fingers slick it smooth.

And oh the snow, webbed from air's nothingness:
its drift, its soft insistence
its crystal facets scattering light
while days open and close
folding into the dark.

# Kilrane

**Wendy McGrath**

mistake Kilrane for a storm eye
where sand and water burr stone
and seaweed boas document tide

its bitter cold denied today
we rush the freezing waves
breathless in Jupiter's wake

rung out and racing hard from shore
past unripe burrs on thorny green
these ditch pineries will boast tokens

when ripe and plucked sweet berries
each sweet berry sweet purple sweet
will sate our salt-borne thirst

# THE SOUND OF CELLULOSE

**Geoffrey Nilson**

I am a human in love with the wind.
basic need for movement, affinity for recklessness
I pin back my ears & eat the combinations.

carve the breath from my chest, rough rock
medallion with inscriptions of gravity
cuts over cuts, the healing we call growth.

the mud spatters my shins, rough earth
tender with moss, living in careful complexity
sunlight open to the branches, faded basin.

hold on for dear through the descent
my fear between all things like air, running.
death, like life, only travels in one direction.

will I live long enough to hear the end
of poetry? will it come when no ears listen?
a bough of feathers given willingly.

what does the bicycle say to my legs?
nothing—it's too busy spinning its wheels.
the poem cranks a tire in the mud

I slide into the corner before the chaos
as if I meant to, freewheel a kinetic flash of love.
from the saddle at speed the trees moan

more than ever, tones of faith & devotion.
read somewhere they have their own languages—
I'm not surprised. I've heard them singing.

# DRIFT

**Nancy Pagh**

*Lepas anatifera* Linnaeus

In an enclosed pool near the marina, my young instructor scattered a series of sinking squares—unused rubber heels—in the shallow end, then retired to a pink-striated cabana. "Puts face in water." Check. "Holds breath under water." Check on the form for my parents. But in his absence, I'd gathered them all with my toes.

>    gray drizzle
>    gray bay
>    gray driftwood
>    interspaced

Nobody tells the best part of obesity. Fat floats. In lakes and inlets all along the coast I stretched full length—back arched, arms crossed behind my head. I put my face in sky and breathed.

>    goose walking
>    goose flying
>    same goose?

# THE BIRDS, BUTTERFLIES AND SNAKES OF HAMILTON, ONTARIO: AN EXCERPT FROM *NEEDLEMINER*

**Gary Barwin**

1.

we are for the chuck-will's-widow
the horned grebe
the fulvous whistling-duck
for looking directly into the semi-palmated plover
for the shearwater
for the lazuli bunting
the razorbill and the canvasback redhead
for the ferruginous hawk
and the black-crowned night heron
for black-legged kittiwakes in general
and cerulean warblers specifically
for recalling the bohemian waxwing and the black rail
for the veery and little blue heron
for the belted kingfisher and the least bittern
for the american redstart and wilson's phalarope
for the black-necked stilt
the long-billed curlew
the greater yellowlegs
the muddy godwit
for the turnstone red knot and the pectoral sandpiper
for the storm petrel
the glossy ibis
for the great cormorant
for living in madness


2.

there was
a silver-spotted skipper
in which

snowberry clearwing
tortoiseshell risen
cabbage white

where northern cloudywing
hairstreak
eastern pine elfin

where mourning cloak
broken dash
silver blue

where little wood satyr
underwing
silver-bordered fritillary

where checkerspot
mulberry
hobomok skipper

where glassywing
broken dash
american snout

where dun skipper
question mark
red-spotted purple

where hummingbird clearwing
pawpaw sphinx
little yellow

who brush-footed
silver-spotted
who snowberry blinded

who clouded
silver-bordered
who great-spangled

who tawny-edged
duskywinged
who painted

who grey
who common
who pearly-eyed

who broad-winged
two-spotted
who giant

silver-spotted skipper

3.

ring-necked the milk snake
is mud puppy
redbelly
oh what the garter

red-backed
four-toed
blue-spotted
ribboned smooth green

oh what the ring-necked
milk snake
all redbelly garter
oh ribboned mud puppy

oh four-toed
blue-spotted
never ribboned
oh all smooth green

oh

# CALL IT WILD SWIMMING

**Beth Kope**

In deep
kick at coils of watershield and coontail
that hide catfish or cutthroat
long as scaled babies.

Call it wild swim and dive
to submerged logs'
blanched limbs.

Enter murk, a colder territory,
where crimes drownproof
and I wear the lake's pelt.

Slips of dragonflies navigate
the lake's surface by shadow zip.
I am blue split with longing,

I am water, container,
colliding with porous signals, liquid
within and without.

# GRANDMOTHER RIVER

**Solveig Adair**

before she died we
drove the car out to the place
where three rivers stilled
and joined and I helped
her pass down to the shore's edge
her heartbeat as wild
as a bird beneath my thumb

salmon rose before
us   thick and red as old   blood
hemorrhage beneath
the skin of the earth   the waves

she knelt there   her hands
joined with the water   arteries
thick with fish and   death
of the transient   salmon
flesh returned to purity

before she died she
knelt in the river   and when
I blinked there was no
distinction between her and
the water            body
fed by veins and arteries
wild as water returning
always to the   heart

# Sounds a River Makes

**Claire Caldwell**

Gas leak, ventilator, bear clicking its teeth.

Twelve hundred caribou hooves on frost.

Lips around bottle, bottle clinking

on bar. Rattling aspen, dusky grouse,

sheets drying outside. Grandmas

stuffing envelopes in a high school gym.

Sex in a sleeping bag, house on fire.

A children's choir after one kid

has fainted.

# GREEN RAIN

**Terri Brandmueller**

When Howard Hughes
camped out on the top floor
of that Vancouver hotel
wearing Kleenex boxes
for slippers
washing his hands
20 times an hour
did he look out through the film of rain
to the mucky lagoon below
where ducks stopped
for stale bread

did he see these refugees from the Pacific flyway:
the iridescence of the mallard drake's head
the brilliant speculum of the green-winged teal
dazzling in the bobbing black cove where
dabbling puddle ducks squonk and burble
splashing noisily for scraps and crusts
while placid mallard hens and nervous widgeons
wait for the day's farinaceous flotsam

did he spy the diving ducks—
skunk-headed surf scoters
skid stopping out in the deep green
rafts of velvety black scaups and buffleheads
goldeneyes and downy eiders
disappearing in unison
to resurface as synchronized swimmers

did he spot the grounded Canada goose
spitting in her mossy nest of wet leaves

did he long to ditch those
crazy Kleenex boxes in the white hotel lobby
run barefoot over the grimy parking lot

to the slimy banks of the lagoon
and with duck shit and soggy breadcrumbs
oozing up between his toes
his hermit's beard plastered over his heart
stand in the shadow of steel and glass while
long veils of green rain
washed him clean?

# LATE SEPTEMBER

**Robert Boates**

*for Brian*

Driving north to Athabasca
through seasons fighting
for conquest of an afternoon.
A crack across the windshield
suggests lightning; a bolt sealed
in a paperweight like a scorpion,
its tail poised to strike.

The day is full of slaughter.
Sleet-covered cattle wait to be led
to market. Deer evade searching eyes.
Smaller animals remain concealed, for death
wears wings and is always swift.

We are small beneath this sky,
travelling toward the horizon.
That rainbow in the distance,
a sickle, a promise.

# Judd Beach

**Bren Simmers**

let us walk the sandy trails through spotted alder trunks, the flush of salmonberry,
our blood 92% water, the river here long before we were born and long after
blossoms, hot pink, blurred zing of hummingbirds darting back and forth through
animal and ancestor, the river recycled into cloud, the same water falls as rain over
the live corridor, over banked jumps built for BMX, the loose cluster of teens
sticky sweet cottonwood buds that unfurl tender green, transform to gold filigree
spilling the banks, cutting a new channel, the river, time itself, our lives rushing past
wild, feral. add your track to the wet sand: dog, coyote, eagle, parentheses of elk,
sometimes slow, sometimes surging, flood warning, spilling its banks brown and fast,
bear scat come salmon run, socket-less skulls, stench of writhing corpses, maggots
just downstream of where coho fry hide in shaded overhangs. what makes a life.
vertebrae scatter in the fist-sized cobbles, basalt and andesite covered with slime
kids splashing in the shallows, the river crystal clear or cloudy with glacial silt
and later, rocks capped with snow rising like dough, the river a place of renewal,
seasons blur into years: flooded trails that horsetails drink, pinball flight of swallows
return, the source.

# OBSERVATION

**Derk Wynand**

How the light breaks when it does.

How the eye takes in the light breaking.

How the brain corrects the upside-down image
if that's what it does.

How the mountain's reflection on the lake water
resembles the mountain.

How you become less and less certain.

If you throw a stone, how the water ripples.
How the reflected mountain becomes rippling water only.

How the water becomes smooth again.

How your uncertainty returns if it does so.

How your brain tricks your body
into thinking itself absent.

How water must do just that for stone.

earth mother's birth tears
seep through mountain gravel rock
return home to sea

**Karen Charleson**,
Ayyi'saqh, Hesquiat Harbour

# II. Movement

Earth's water is always in movement, and the natural water cycle, also known as the hydrologic cycle, describes the continuous movement of water on, above, and below the surface of the Earth. Water is always changing states between liquid, vapor, and ice, with these processes happening in the blink of an eye and over millions of years.

**—The Fundamentals of the Water Cycle**

I've known rivers:
I've known rivers ancient as the world and older than the flow of human blood in
　human veins.
My soul has grown deep like the rivers.
**—Langston Hughes**

And what is the name for the movement we make when
we wake, swiping hand or claw or wing across our face, like trying
to remember a path or a river we've only visited in our dreams?
**—Aimee Nezhukumatathil**

# WHERE

## Katherena Vermette

not up in the groomed grass
of the pretty park

not in the hilly bush
high with growth and garbage

not kneeling
on those polished pews

not even where the upright stones
bruise the earth


not at the street where
the fake flowers faded long ago

or where the wounds open
and cry out every night

not on the bridge where
some went

or at old wood dock where
others were taken


but here near this last bend
in the river

here where the trees break off
and their leaves dance high with song

here where the water licks the sky
like smoke

and the concrete is so old
and smoothed as rock


here where the dock broke off
and the edge is low

where the wind moves quick in
and long out

there is still tobacco
and there is still fire

here with the river is where
I will remember

# GENIUS LOCI
**xavier o. datura**

*for S'ólh Téméxw (the traditional territories of the Stó:lō)*

out in the valley
plump drupelets fall into the thicket
the butterflies are always drunk.

disturbed plots beneath the powerlines
become breeding grounds for
noxious children.

common broom supplants the old gods
dragging golden knuckles across
the flat-lying meadow.

drones round here drive pimped trucks
furnishing the colony with blue-stained
beetle kill.

the mussels are all sedentary these days
no oolichan left to grease
the ancient gears.

wapato once grew in abundance here but
who gives a fuck about swamp potatoes
with these supersized fries.

they say the one who made this place
his people, his sky-born wife
were created right over there.

on that hill with the fancy properties
with the aggregate potential
of everything.

# Riven

**Laura Apol**

> *Because, of course, we can't bring back the past;*
> *we can't bring back the dead.*
> —Anne Michaels

This is the way water goes:

rain filters through fields, rivulets
run the ravine     to the stream,
to the river, to the Great Lake.
Follow that path; like time, it flows
only one       way. Yet

each year the salmon
reverse,

come in from the hugeness
of water,       fight the current
toward the creek, past fallen
branches, clots of twigs and rocks
and flats;

flip and flash their way over gravel,
bodies pink, then spotted
with decay. They are death, they are

life,       they are food
for scavenging eagles and foxes,
coyotes and owls, food for their own
      spawn;
spawning, spawned—is this

a story of hope or loss? Is memory
*in* or *of* water? Day
after day, the fall foliage
thins,       yellow confetti shed
into the stream—

as if the Lake,
as if the river; as if the fox and owl;
as if the fish bones and the rainbow
skins and the empty
eyes

fed and were fed by the journey
              home
—as if the past is the future
and the ravaged salmon
           reach it—

this rock-strewn ravine, slicked
with rain; this putrid stream, bright-
        gilded with dying
leaves.

# Bypass Project

**gillian harding-russell**

In the truck's industrial roar
the savannah sparrow changes gears—
his mating call needing to be heard
above the ruckus, a piping trill

that soars
low notes that pour
under the mammoth drone
parked in a thistle and alfalfa
field, raw earth wounds dug out
where the fox tails and wild oats
and daisy previously swayed
in a slight wind, and a mate
amidst a buffet of seeds waits.

Rising concrete arches over
the prairie
hugeness bridges the sky
monumental as the pyramids
over the mud-rucked hardpack
and man-made hill—
we've been to the moon
and back, and there's nothing more
important than here.

The construction workers wear hard hats
and work overtime: the overpass for a province
that trades with the world
the work welcomes, helps families
and breaks backs, all-night staff rushes
to meet a deadline as the crane rises
and the shovel drops.

Though what when the small brown bird pines
without an audible mate?

Though what when the sun scorches
the back of the land, brown as a burnt loaf
already?

Though what when the sun like any old star
burns up—a handful of stardust, the heart
inside fresh raindrops
                              in the artificial dark
where new life will crop up?

# Elaho

**Trevor Carolan**

Trucking thru Squamish River country in a
dinged-up logger's crummy,
we bump thru closest thing to the Golden Triangle
past clear-cuts, big stump bone-yards.
Lucky from the Wilderness Committee says,
    "You'd never find this place on your own..."

We pitch camp on a river bar, keeping eye out
for big fish-eaters—
    Elder Brother Bear, his kinfolk.
Glaciers to the north   south   west
big peaks    ancient massive trees;
timber wolves howl in moonlight,

hair stands on the back of our necks.
Delgawmuukw court case gives legal title back
to aboriginal First Nations.
Now, there's new scrapes with Big Lumber
and eco-warriors get beaten-up by corporate thugs.
Here and there though, a butt-salvage team

still splits cedar shakes in the deadlands.
John Clark leads us in past waterfalls,
the way he's done for forty years
through Devil's Club, valerian root,
    to learn herb-picking on the mount,
    this pocket meadow the Grizzlies love,

        paying acute attention
            to simply everything.
          Suddenly we're *here.*

# HERRING SEASON, 1992

**Emily Olsen**

there's never been so many men
lusting over such quick fish
fifteen-minute money-making
gumboots and cigarettes

coastal towns
gone beer and treachery
young girls escorted home
(made to feel like visitors)

the wharves clink and creak
boat-wakes rattle
the very bones
of quiet morning fog

soon
cash, gluttony

Later, the full-bellied salmon
reach their spawning ground
find stream and forest
parched and brittle
scales flake off
and sink to sediment

# The Promise of Rivers Shanty

**Harold Rhenisch**

There is the Deadman, where the stone flowed like fire,
and black Vidette Lake, at the centre of the world,
among crumbling islands the moon blew in from the sea.
There is the Bonaparte, thin stream in red stone,
and Pavillion Lake, daughter of Mars. There is the Fraser,
stream of pit houses and smoke shacks, draining the sap
of the sky and the silver of the moon, the rain
turned into a ladder for salmon on the road of the stars.
There is the sea's throat gone to raw smoke. There is Fish Lake and Big Creek
with their loons and their reeds. There is Lac des Bois
in its bowl of sparrows and thatched grass, and Beecher Lake,
gravel cup in a shaman's sky, and Hohium,
where the thunder strikes, and Big Bar, where the glaciers died.
These are the waters that flow down from the Mother.
These are the ocean the clouds have lifted to the air. There is the Kettle,
where stars slip through the grass dance of the ponderosas,
with their white tails and their deep thoughts frozen in bone.
There is McClean Creek, that shifts past the dog
that waits still for the salmon to breach Okanagan Falls,
and the Sinlahekin with its white grass and frog-faced moon croaking out song;
there is the Mahood, where cedars drink stone, and the Canim,
which catches the wind; and there is the Fraser's songline,
the San Jose, Lac La Hache, the Walker, the Bridge,
Horse Lake, Lac des Roches, and the Thompson's bright rapids,
in their bed of horsetails and herons against the wall of the world.
There is the Horsefly, nosing the gold of ghost rivers
that the world followed when it returned to the people from the cold.
There is the Columbia that carries the dust of Black Sage and Vantage
down the red ochre road to Steamboat Slough and Cape Disappointment,
where it spills its dust into the Pacific's chalk maw.
There are the lost bowls of Celillo, at the crossroads, and Bromley,
with its fingertips traced in salmon grease and ochre.
There is the Wenatchee, sister of Eagle and Painted Turtle.
There is the Tulameen, with its flint and platinum gravel,
and White Cliffs, where men turned a handful of dust into a star.

These are the roads the mind travels on its bare feet in the cool of morning,
and there is the Fraser, skein of candlefish and glass,
trail of polished stone and the sheep that follow the sun
through the black bears and thunder of the Nikomen's rapids,
and their hunters who track the wind back up to its floods.
These are the waters that flow through our hands now,
that pool in our lungs and beat in our hearts, and these are the waters
that fill the hollows of our foot taps in the dust of volcanoes
where the earth split and spoke fire. There is the Monte and its cliffs of green glass,
and the Similkameen, that spurns the fast fall to cedars for the long
road through Copper Mountain and the green oxbows at Chopaka,
where a people found their name and the land its own people.
There is the Beef, in its valley of willows, and the Chilcotin,
in its bed of salt. There is Puntzi Lake and its pelicans and soap light,
and the Dean, and its trout rising on evenings in August
to pluck the stars from a still untamed sky.
There is the Tusulko, Blue Canyon Creek, and the Corkscrew:
organ music in the beds of the rivers of ice,
where the stone-footed climb to the end of stone,
where the waters that begin the return from the winter
first feel the winter return. There is Spahats Creek, where stone crumbled,
and Nimpo and Anahim, where stars spawn. There is the Fraser,
that carries the first silver people to quilted clam song.
There is Trout Creek, with its cotton-mouthed shadows,
and the Douglas in its constellations of fescue, caribou and snow.
There are the White Salmon and the Chelan
that catch themselves falling and then gives themselves air,
the white Methow, and the orange Chuckchow,
as shallow as silk being drawn over stones by a wing.
These are the waters that flow through the Mother,
that carry her down, that we drink, that we honour.
There is the star road and the road of the waters—
Scotch Creek Basin and Salmon Creek speaking salt.
There is the Canoe and the Dog, where the land split in two,
and Alkali Lake, Swan Lake and Spring House,
where men gave the wind to horses, and they ran with it
and will never return. There is the Rose, and the Knife, and the Beaver,
the Roe and the Latremouille. These are the waters that bring the sky to us.
This is where the trees come to the shore to drink stone.

There is the Gallagher, where the earth has no floor,
and Klikut, where the earth's thousand eyes look out together,
and the people's people become the green sweat bees with blue
dresses that tend their larvae under hot sand few men can stand.
There is the Goose, the Spqmix, the Duck, and long Kalamalka,
pearls in the throat of the lost seas of the ice.
There is Tuc-el-nuit, Green, Yellow, White, and gasoline-perfumed Osoyoos,
where rattlers swim out from bitter root and stonecrop,
where the rain's people leap from eight inches of living water
into the long run to the sandpipers of the Sakhalin Islands,
as naked as the salt's moon calling them back to the old reds of the Siwash.
This is where we return, where we hear Sen'klip, our ancestor, call,
and on still nights the high song of the aurora,
and the snow underfoot, and the fire and its summer.
These are the round eyes of Sepa, and Succour, and Spring,
this is where their divers wait one afternoon for the ice to green like a leaf's breath,
to the waters that bring us back, again and again,
to the raindrops, the snowflakes, and storm.
These are the children of fire meeting the sea, and waves calling
and calling and calling and calling and calling
for shore. This is the shore. These are the ways
of the water. This is the water in the stone. This
is the song in the stone. This is the stone in the song.

# Swamp Preserve

**Alyse Knorr**

If every new thought has been thought already,
if distance is measured in rain and it rains here
every day, if the man cuts down the ghost iris
because scarcity yields value, if only a year ago
you didn't know my name, if sweat dampens
the hair trailing down your neck, if it rains again
today and starts another fire, if the strangler fig
tightens around the waist of the cypress, then
when will this world end so the new one can begin?

# CROSSING THE TAYLOR BRIDGE

**Rebekah Rempel**

Ice fog looms above the valley, huge
as a blue whale's breath,

the Peace River a pewter
ache against the snow.

My tires growl on the metal
grating—the sound an animal makes

when threatened. Ahead,
flames gush from flare stacks

at the sour gas plant, spilling
paths of light across the river, as if

I could walk there. And upstream,
a dam slowly builds—valley waiting

to be flooded, water forced
down a man-made throat.

Sometimes
I look for hope—

in the mule deer
stepping tender-hoofed

along the shore, pine and spruce
staggering over the hills,

magpies flinging their newsprint wings
against the cold. I look and try to find

comfort in this: despite us,
they have always known

how to survive.

# FLYING RIVER

**Alisa Gordaneer**

Potentially radical: green plants shape weather, shake up rainfall.
Plants over here influence plants over there;
forests influence weather.

Leaves split water, stitch hydrogen, oxygen, carbon
virtually all life molecular wizardry: stomata of
a single leaf, 1 million structures.

Forests move water inconceivably. The Amazon
makes its own storms, wind currents
transport forest-driven flying rivers.

Consider cause and effect: it's wet
because there are forests.
Carbon dioxide fluxes the biosphere.

Try foresting the Arctic
an expansion of northern spruce forests
encroaching deciduous, birch or aspen.

Ice to melt on a feedback loop, amplifying
North America, Europe, and Asia into forest again,
exaggerated greening farmland returns.

Energy, atmospheric currents
redistributed to the north, a distant mechanism.
Such remote triggers influence the novelty.

Forests did the influencing. In the tree cover,
losses are part of our world. A provocative wake-up
to rewriting the maps of too many disparate mechanisms.

How much rain will fall?
Signals emerge amid pushes and pulls.
One thing is clear: influence is felt.

# THE POND

**Zachariah Wells**

*for Andy*

The pond was first a creek,
percolating into a reek-
rich bog. Then came dumptrucks
and dozers, to heap shale and rock
across the creek's
path and pack
it tight, a pale blue PVC pipe stuck
into the dyke
like a periscope stack
to drain the eventual flood. Trickle
by drop the muddy tub filled. It took
six weeks.
A haphazard dock,
cobbled together with planks
and peeled cedar trunks
for pilings, was sunk
into red mud. Finally, the creeping flood broke
the overflow's rim to slake
the parched bed of the brook.
Once sediment settled down into the muck,
the waters cleared, it was time to take stock.
And so, the pond was stocked
with rainbows raised in a tank,
but their ranks
shrank
and shrank.
I caught the last one, his once-iridescent flank
blotched and pocked
by fungus and wounds, stubborn underslung jaw hooked
up like a gaff.
                    Still, the pond teems, surface pinked
by local speckled,
rising to flies in the dusk
as I watch from my spot on the rot-patched dock.

# Estuarine

**Karen Chester**

First Wolf

There is an amber orb
where once was moon
a reflection of dust, of star, of knowing.
Soft ear, sharp muzzle
a tilting back, closing of eyes.
A vagal chorus.

Second Wolf

Lean and limber, Wolf slips wetly
across a bed of eel grass.

His stride, eyes, hungry.
A long wait for a few fish bones, a half-eaten crab.
Raven keeps vigil, hopes for leftovers.

First Wolf

There is a cold that Second Wolf cannot know
where mountains meet sky, the gods
the humans—puppet hearts in the stars.
Soft rain, sharp cry: one Wolf
then the other, across the catenary.
Diamond dust.

Second Wolf

A chill creeps in: wet fur, wet feet
and a belly full of hunger.

Eel grass as bed, as nest: for moon snails, herring.
But not for Wolf, who makes a sharp right.

First Wolf

Watches. Like Raven. Or Hermes.

Second Wolf

Fir needles, soft, Wolf slows
his hunger hollow, a copper bell.
Circling, circling, circling, spine against cedar, nose in tail
Wolf dreams salmon dreams—moon in sky: salmon eye
moon on water: swimming silver; distant bell: fish at dawn.

# HOMECOMING

**David Martin**

We're closing in on the toe
of Athabaska glacier, trailing
chatter marks and striations.

The ice advances and recedes
each day, smeared in rusty
microbes that siphon albedo.

This field is a pollutant
cold storage, inheritance
stilled in high-tide breakers.

Our tread-marks sinter
the snow, fusing flakes
by evicting blisters of air.

We sidestep moulins that
seduce our path and strive
to devour another hiker.

Beneath the firn's seal,
split-leg molecules of DDT
camouflage, sweating it out.

Entombed in a wintry womb,
these microscopic seeds pine
to teem back into mainstreams.

Prodigal isomers remind me
this chemical bond is for life:
Nerve signals crowed open,

eggshells leached of calcium,
sperm tranquilized, and
cancer frenzied in the liver.

When the ice at last ablates
and meltwater punctures
the terminal moraine's lip,

human residues will lie
as stowaways sewn in
outwash, nested in water tables.

We stand on the frozen grade
knowing the next snowfall
will scumble our tracks,

while molecular scrimmage
seethes in the glacial cage,
primed to dog its way home.

# FISH LADDER

**John Pass**

Yes, yes, the practicalities, take steps
or lose the biggest runs on earth come through
Hell's Gate, the spawn-rich possibilities
of waterfall-blocked Stikine tributaries.
But how we love the overlook

from where we blast our rights of way
above the torrent, and the view through glass
of resting pools for their ascent

we made. And this too, most
especially this: ubiquitous
freeze-frame of leaping fish
(those Tlingit dead seeking ice country

f-stopped at Super Natural
BC) icon of brochure

and wish as shrouded as St. Joan's
first putting on bright steel at Blois
or Scott's setting foot in Antarctica.

Antipodes. Limbless, errant muscle in the air
shook pennant of its element
held proud above a consequence

delayed, ever
suspended
            is what we dream
is what we touch each other with
like touching wood.

# BUTE INLET

## Zoë Landale

The river says: water parts air the way old flesh slides
from bones. Coincides. High up the bank you bend
to an extended line of flotsam, what are these grey arrows

the size and texture of a narrow boot toe?
You flinch when you see back-facing serrations. Teeth.
Then you know: salmon noses transformed to rubber,

embers of the eyes long gone, cheek plates
giant scales. Ankle deep, these are the lavish dead.
You pick one up, translate detail as well your

own internal shift between *before*, seeing the heads'
shapes as abstraction and beautiful, and the flinch.
Being led to see closely is a form of loving.

Seasons mean a live ring rotates between inlet and icefield.
Winters, the river rearranges the valley floor
with the peeled delicacy of the inevitable, say a dam

buckling, the trickle turning to a slam of water,
utter disintegration, only here is just riprap and roads,
the wisdom of gravel bars which forgive alterations

though they don't forget aberration, the river's
variableness and turning. Yearning to see grizzlies amble
onto gravel bars and scoop out slivers of light; salmon.

August penstemmon bloom. Within the ring, fireweed and thistle
seeds ascend in linked white clusters, buoyant as prayers,
an epistle to the glaciers; the days exceed yearning.

# WILD PLACE

**Christine Smart**

> *Art in a time of radical loss is an elegy.*
> *It teaches us how to mourn...*
> —Alison Hawthorne Deming

I. First Wild Place

The creek below the farm: secret, separate,
muddy spring snowmelt— a river—
rapids roared, banks eroded,
overflowed and flooded fields.

*Stay clear*, mother warned: slippage, drowning.
I dawdled at the edge, roughly
a lie, no time for play on that farm, no running
wild, mud-streaked and free, always
held back, standing on the brink.

The creek called me
to play, water burbled, I jumped
stepping stones
slippery in shade or sun,
and dappled light.

Banks scoured and damp,
birds warbled and frogs croaked
I splashed among reeds.

The creek dissected the farm
nameless source, imagined destination,
the boundary fence: barbed wire.

Long hot days, summer sun-dried,
cow pies and hoof-print sludge

the log bridge decayed, the wild
wetland, a hide-away escape

the snaking gulley under sugar maples,
in cool damp dark.


II. Last Wild Place, circa 2050

The creek below the farm
dry, oh so dry,
the log bridge collapsed, no gap
to fall through, no
red maples, the gulley parched
and choked with thistles.

A west wind blows cinders,
corn crops withered, soil depleted.
The sky, a great blue basket
of heat, no clouds or thunderheads.

The creek bed echoes rumbling,
the smooth rocks speak
silent tears.


III. How did I get back here?

A long hot trek, crossing
the country from west to east on foot, I saw no
ancestors only tracks
but no trains, highways and gravel roads,
no cars or trucks. Airport
runways invaded,
dandelions in the cracks.

Round stepping-stones
stuck in the dry
creek bed, weathered, worn
weeping dust,
fossils: small signals
remember cool water, flooding
spring run off.

Quiet, oh so quiet, burned dry, I found water
gushing from my eyes,
the path rough and ragged, I could do
nothing.

# Lost Stream

**Fiona Tinwei Lam**

Forgotten one, you remember what you were:
mossy banks, fringes of fern, rivulets, riffles,
cool passage for salmon. On a map
of old streams spilling out to the strait
you were one of hundreds
of capillaries threading through earth
muscled with rock, lavished with forest.
Then the city donned concrete
masks, civilized grids. Smothered
into park, you were culverted, diverted, yoked,
locked into pipes while we romped above.
But you refuse to be choked
under clearcut, brushcut tracts. Playing fields
soak back into marsh. Bog rises through playground.
One by one, oaks topple in sodden soil,
upended roots like tangled claws.
Submerged roads around you
ripple in wind. Water above seeks
water below. Deep underground,
you gurgle, chortle, ready to rise.

# THIS POEM IS ONE PILLAR

**Kelly Shepherd**

> *The Goddess ... has squeezed herself into her magpie suit.*
> —Harold Rhenisch

Although it enjoys high sunshine hours,
Edmonton's weather is often changeable.

The trees with their interlocking fingers
form an archway over the road and the bus

drives under the trees, which are clouds.
Trees without leaves or blossoms are still

clouds: they resemble clouds, reach
with their dry hands for clouds, drink

from clouds, exhale clouds. Clouds are canvases
for sunsets and sunrises, front covers of star-maps,

water-vapour cartographies of impossible
colours. Cathedrals have pillars,

which are trees, that hold up cloud
-shaped domes of sky. People go inside

to worship or cry or pray, in other words to imagine
they are outside, under clouds. Next to me on the bus

her hand with faded tattoos
the moon and stars.

# Excerpt from *TreeTalk: Winnipeg*

**Ariel Gordon**

"A big old specimen will have about 1 million leaves or an acre of leaf surface, and will cast a pool of shade 100 feet in diameter."—Donald Culross Peattie

How do you know a tree?
You are three times as tall as me, double my age.
I can't help but maybe I won't hurt, this paper, this string.

SECRET: I used to think that there was such a thing as an acorn tree. Until I was 27.

The breeze filters through.
Billows of talk, the passage of cars.
The leaves. The leaves, arrayed…

"Elm leaves decompose rapidly, and are high in potassium and calcium, making American Elm a 'soil-improving' species."—*Plants of the Western Boreal Fores*t

His shirt open, a scar stands out on his belly,
showing the trajectory of a blade
as he bends to write: *This bird can sing.*

Open. Open. The sky grey, the humidity high. Garage sales down side streets. Vines climbing brickwork. Brown sparrows & orange lights.

I can't stop staring at the extension cord, up in a branch.
The tree wired. In a few hours,
those lights will come on like fireflies, like stars.

SECRET: I'm scared of falling back into old habits.

An assembly of middle-aged trees, a chorus.
Taking a stand. Roots infiltrating below, branches reaching above.
Filling the sky. Leafing out.

"Is an elm tree a hardwood or softwood? Do elm trees grow fast? How long does an elm live for?"—*People Also Ask*, Google.com

Leaning towards the shade. The trees wading pools of coolness. Shallow relief.

Rain-dated. Sunday-ed.
Weather-delayed. Traffic-calmed.
Garage-saled.

The insistence of trees. Dying: branches falling into traffic, leaves on windshields. Danger trees. Windowmakers.

> We had a "Mom"
> who lived down the street,
> and she was so sweet
> We are here to remember her
> Her life was like this tree. (heart)
> 1921–2017

"Elm wood is used for dry-goods barrels, boxes, crates, furniture, flooring, panelling, caskets, and boat-building."—*Plants of the Western Boreal Forest*

The tree fills out. A fullness of words. A leafy manuscript.
A streetwise folio.

Carpe Tree-m—Seize the leaves.
re-foliate—re-populate

Veni vidi foliage.

A man with a magnificent wolf's tail clipped to his belt. A streak of dyed hair gleams as he disappears down the street, sunglasses mirroring his eyes.

I am sessile. Sidewalked. Sidelined.
So I make lists. A hierarchy of needs.
A laundry list of complaints.
After all, I'm attempting a canopy of poems.

# THE WHIRLWIND QUESTIONS BURNCO ROCK PRODUCTS LTD.

(regarding its environmentally-certified pit mine which will dredge 20 million tonnes of sand and gravel from the McNab Creek Estuary in Howe Sound, B.C.)

**Susan Alexander**

> *Look at Behemoth, which I made just as I made you.*
> —Job 40.15

Where were you when the peaks climbed
high above the sound? Can you speak
with a voice that quells the Squamish blow?
Is it you who tilts the waterskins, who swells
the stream into cascades, who calls home
the coho, dog, and pink? Can you vault
like the rainbow? Or scent creek pebbles,
rushed by earth's magnetic pull? Have you
offered meat for cougar, bobcat, bear?
For the eagle and the goshawk?
Can you hold this one small bud, forge
the arbor-vitae? Will you live the cedar's
thousand years? Have you shaped an egg
into red-legged frog or rough-skinned newt?
Does your body snare carbon
in sea sedge meadows? Have you heard
the elk calve under the canopy, her twins
hidden beneath the thimbleberry bush?
Have you the heron's skill, her stillness?
Can you, like the salamander,
manufacture a missing limb?

# EXCERPT FROM *BEHOLDEN*

## Rita Wong and Fred Wah

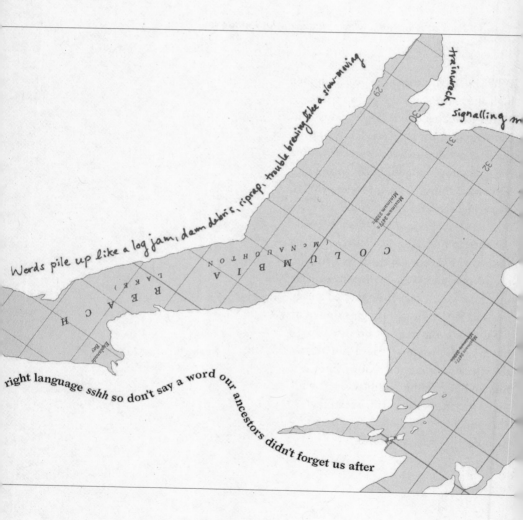

Words pile up like a log jam, dam debris, riprap, trouble breaking like a slow-moving trainwreck, signalling m

right language sshh so don't say a word our ancestors didn't forget us after

ough unless they are put to the purpose of making a home for elk, caribou, bears, beavers, imagine salmo

H

ll remember the future ghosts of ourselves gathered to collect promised pay back but we get data instead

36°

37

when she swam here for thousands of years, before the long, loud, loaded train rumbling through the

COLUMBIA REACH

of bull trout beneath the Reach the kokanee hear the muffled rumbling of the train nothing comes

at the bottom

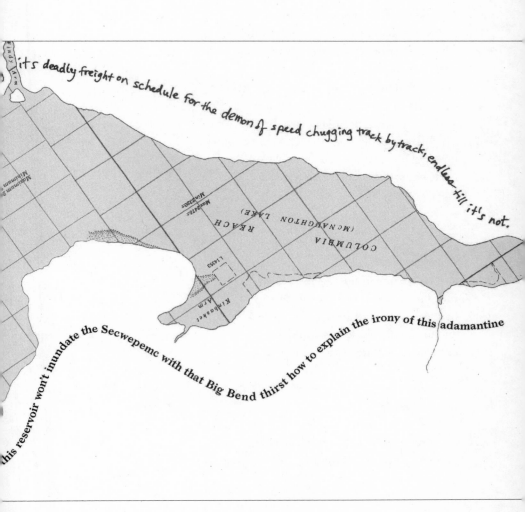

it's deadly freight on schedule for the demon of speed chugging track by track, endless till it's not.

this reservoir won't inundate the Secwepemc with that Big Bend thirst how to explain the irony of this adamantine

# DON RIVER, CROSSINGS AND EXPEDITIONS

**Anita Lahey**

1.

A worker honeybee from the abandoned apiary
in the cottage backyard of famed naturalist
Charles Sauriol motors over the riverbank and plunges
into a wall of black swallowwort. One more
newfangled post-industrial invader. (It straitjackets
trees and strangles dogs.) Bring this mighty forager
a blossom all native and nectar-y, bring it
a highrise of goldenrod, an eighteenth-century
bustle of milkweed. On the double. (Where
is the ghost of Elizabeth Simcoe
when you need her?)

2.

A skate blade loops
and swirls, unwinding clarity,
movement, joy. When the divide
between water and air is cold-packed
and unmistakable, forces and states
of being may unite. An ancient

corn cob, a dropped
fishing spear, rings fanning
from a cupped palm. Ripples
of a circumspect gaze. Undercurrents
of hoeing, hewing, humming.

3.

Do giant slushy pops still exist
or have these plastic Slurpee cups
the size of watering cans been rolling
in brush by the skunk cabbage
at the Todmorden Mills wildflower preserve

housing ants, rain, mosquitoes
and spiders since 1982?


4.

The official, thirtyish, bristled chin, wades in,
angling for a grip on the fourth
body this season. *Maybe the poor
chump's better off, you know?* His black
boot, a slime-slick rock, careening and fingers
flung through reedy air. Steady, okay,
wait—two hands holding zippo, nada—
Was there a splash? His walkie-talkie's
gone under to join what fell and sank
with buddy from the bridge. Up there,
his partner awaits confirmation,
gloved fingers on the railing, round
black speaker at her ear. Give her
a Luminous Veil. Give her a single
malt, neat. Give her a moment
alone with this feat of engineering
and its larger-than-life legacy.
She wants a word.

5.

Capt. Hugh Richardson's rages and bellows,
caught on a putrid 1834 wind, rising
from the deck of his grounded
vessel at the mouth—
*The destroying cancer! Destructive industry!*—
still fury and eddy with gull screeches
over the head of a repatriated wood duck
traversing the greasy pools
of Keating Channel. (The captain
curses the Don's impassable silt,
not the tanneries, abattoirs,
paper mills, flour mills, lumber mills,
lantern factories and cattle fields
from which it cascaded.)

6.

That particular night heron spent
two motionless hours perched on a post
poking through the surface near a crack
in the concrete that encases the lower bank.
Its grey-blue bill trained on water, head feathers
ever-so-slightly rearranged by the breeze. Mourners
in the hundreds were drifting downriver
aboard kayak, canoe, rowboat, raft, re-enacting
the Funeral for the Don. The chief keener,
mid-wail, erect in the bow, spotted
the stock-still bird. Fell
mute. The heron's intentions
were clear. People stared. Some leaned
so far over to peer (like the bird)
directly into the stink, their
vessels began to list.

7.

Sauriol's memories waft downstream
from the Forks, interrupting the flow
on the DVP. Nostrils lift,
ears twitch. Vehicles (not
canoes) bob and sway:

*the scent of the balm of Gilead—*
*the sweet tremolo of a saw-whet owl—*
*the sad trilling of American toads, so plaintive—*
*dozens of eastern bluebirds dropped*
*from a sky as blue as their wings—*

8.

A Rob Ford bobblehead is wedged
in the Y of a staghorn sumac branch
near a patch of graffiti—*I be creepin'*
*while you sleepin'*—on the underside
of the Dundas Street bridge. The sumac

were planted along the once-bleak bank
by sweat-streaked, jean-clad champions
of native species. How long before a
high wind or passing cyclist knocks
the doll free? Its painted-on eyes,
the rerouted shore: now you
see it, now you don't.

9.

A dusty labourer from the brickworks,
dragging on a smoke; a boy
felling a cedar for his latest
ingenious lean-to; an afterschool
trio hugging armloads of trilliums;
buddy, down on his luck, come
all the way from Nova Scotia to erect
a sheet-metal shack on the Flats.
This ghostly gang follows the river's
forgotten, curlicue shoreline, seen
only by owls and bats, reminiscing,
foraging, speculating on what's
yet to float their way, or
surge on by.

10.

Taylor regards the clump
of promising valley clay in his palm.

From the protective shade of oaks,
Simcoe turns his gaze on a stand of pine,
sees masts for ships of war.

Davies takes a pig for a country walk.
Gooderham inspects his windmill's lazily turning blades.
Scadding lays a celery trench, mulches
a bed for tender asparagus shoots.

Gardiner scales a backyard fence to scramble
down the valley. He scrapes his ankles
on raspberry canes, tramples
asters, maps out where
to blast the hill and shove
the river over.

11.

I don't know what to tell you
about life along the Don. It troubles me
to imagine its wild, abundant, free-
flowing past, and how the forms of survival
I was taught to practice have left it
like a dirty, sodden rag. The year I was 22
I crossed it twice a day, sometimes more,
by bicycle, subway, streetcar. On foot,
a friend at my side. We were
cub reporters, I'd taken a call, heard
news meant only for me. He unpeeled
me from my desk to walk me home.
I might have looked down as we crossed,
vaguely noted the familiar, brown trickle
in its trench. I didn't think of the Don
as a waterway, a succession of histories,
an altered form. The valley was
forbidding, unknowable; to live on
its eastern flank was to score
an arresting view. That morning
I crossed the river one kind of person;
I returned used-up, hollow, littered
with debris, dismal as the Don
but still moving, this way
and that, without
apparent design, braced
for my own Improvement Plan. I was due
to be channelled and dredged.

12.

An empty mickey, lid tight, bobs
and meanders, sunlight pooling
in its thick, clear glass.

A corroded nine-volt settles in silt,
kicking up a tiny, temporary, unseen cloud.

The blackbirds' *conk-la-rees*
ricochet from willow to willow
skipping over a log so tattered and forlorn
it can never have stood and splayed
into branches and offshoots,
bright green leaves.

13.

Ah, here she is, Elizabeth Simcoe's ghost—
she's commandeered an abandoned canoe—
Canada geese are splashing and bathing—
she's giddy with swamp gases,
summoning loons.

14.

A Tyee noses upstream, dodging
cigarette butts, coffee cup lids, Styrofoam
crumbs and shards of iPhone
packaging through waters
too warm and up, at intermittent
weirs, precisely, scientifically
angled ladders.

This single-minded chief of all
salmon no way no how voyageured
from the Pacific to this concoction
of road salt and fertilizer, storm sewer
outflow and emptied toilet tanks
propelled by its own fins. No sir. It was

caught, flown over mountains and prairies,
poured into lake water, transformed
into sport for eager anglers.

Ladies and gentlemen of the post-glacial,
post-agrarian, post-Victorian, post-pastoral,
post-industrial, post-landfill, post-
radical-environmental-activist—
ladies and gents of the new-and-improved,
Better-Homes-and-Gardens era of Don River
restoration, please allow me to further describe
the journey undertaken by this pink-scaled
fish of all fishes. This fish

was not game. This Tyee cruised
Lake Ontario's murk, steering clear
of hooks and bait. It smelled
river. Through the port land's rumbles
and slicks, eroded soil grit and driveway sealer
aroma, through beer cans and algae, rainwater
spiked with goose shit, this fish
heard the Don's muted
cough and reeled
in its current. It swims hard and sure—
it belongs here now, it has thrown itself
on the mercy of these ragged, panting waters—
it aims for the source.

# A Feminist Guide to Reservoirs

**Tanis MacDonald**

You want to, but can't
scream at how
we're hated. But you

recall that herons stand
all day in detention
ponds, keep their distance

from other herons. This is not
meant to soothe
but to say herons know

what you're missing.
You have long
suspected capitalism hates

women and geese crave
stormwater
and gender parity.

You walk how you can when you
walk by the reservoir.
*Occupy everything* Dionne Brand said

and the gymnasium of students
rose as one body
to their feet, roaring, and

you thought you had made it,
battered but alive,
to the future. The river

is charged with all the artificial
sweeteners that pass
unaltered through our bodies,

down the sewers and into the river,
molecules of Coke
slipping down the geological

staircase into Lake Erie. Haldimand
Tract, six miles on
both sides of the river, Six Nations

land, and every white person
you know acts
so surprised. *Oh, I didn't*

*know.* One in three
women will be sexually assaulted.

*I was never taught that.*
No one is, until
you are. A creek can

whisper through a city,
a rumour of water
that is water. You cannot

get your breath. Someone
spray-paints
*I Am Broken* on the bunker

over the culvert where
you watch mallards
emerge like a magic

act. You're not, or not
any more
than usual. The gates

open and the river
roars down from where
it's been reserved,

disguised as a pond all
summer. This is
not meant to soothe.

# Respawn

**Heather Fraser**

i.

Snake the drain with a bent wire
Hook a snarl of hair, soap-slick,
flaked with human sediment—
dander, blood, snot

Wrists baptized in greywater
as my ungloved fingers tease the clog loose
The drain belches its relief

My penance for staying too long
under the water, slathering parabens on my skin,
flushing tampons in my youth

Forgive me mother, for I have sinned

ii.

A whole new me coalesces in the sewers,
skin and lard clumping to chicken bones
Rattail of matted hair,
polyethylene beads for eyes,
alligator teeth

I hope the new me does better:
shaves her head to keep her neck cool,
trades shampoo for apple cider vinegar,
digests cruciferous vegetables,
waters her plants

New me born through the estuary's cloaca,
rimed with a vernix of effluent
She rises from the afterbirth knock-kneed,
trembling like a new foal

# Palm Springs

**John Barton**

           why swim through the clear
       waters of those who remain
              thirsty, exhausting the lowered
reservoirs of your strength, the aquifers too
         quickly drained far

            beneath the continent, cavernous
     hearts half empty and ignored

          unreplenished below
this spreading city where stinging
         treated water is stirred by arms and legs
     and a torso, perspiring, you contrive
       to move in toned
         sculpted harmonies

     your butterfly accelerating, lap
after lap, over the startled
       surface of the pool, effortless

         random stone skidding
   across the endless imminence
           of sinking, a fool's
kind of immortality, until
     the reservoirs of your strength
     of their own

         accord, exhaust
   themselves and the body
         thirsts, parched

       wells sunk
   without thought deeper than can be guessed
below the surprised, irrigated, suddenly
       saline wastes of the imagination
         whose forced

bloom has begun to hang
                    anaemic on the espaliered
vine, the aging body a planet
        in denial where from the beginning
                    water is neither

                        created nor destroyed, but now
                no longer falls in plenitude
or fresh, the unforeseen
        subsidences you would today lament
                    were your desire

                not a river diverted
        or dammed, its infernal course, straightened
and constrained, made to wander
                    away from

        glacier and mouth, unable to mingle
its silty origins in the rising
                    oceans where all streams in time
        were once recurrently supposed

                        to expire, but instead what
                remains of the flow
                        pools at some far and temporary
                            oasis where men
        swim in unison, said to be
                        beautiful and impossible
                        to leave

# Not the Lake

**Christine Lowther**

When the creek's *garbledebrook* runs clear, a listener might learn where under the sod the sodding spring springs from. Everybody assumes this is the lake's creek, it emerges from the *lake*—where else? It snakes under the bog, carves through the used-to-be-lush forest, almost suffocates in skunk cabbage quagmires before spilling over boulders, onto limpeted & barnacled shore rocks. There it heightens the cove's complexity, chills & refreshes turgid tides, provides a soundtrack for dipper & resident human. The creek blows bubbles that burst as Nootka roses. The merganser sips sweet estuarine water, tips back her crested head, makes her neck long for the quenching.

The cradled course fills up with rain & discourses more loudly. With winter's roar visitors think they hear a waterfall. Nothing so pompous. The creek doesn't lecture. In summer it withdraws from the conversation, whispers only to self & salamander. But doesn't come from the lake, is not its *offspring*: that's another stream that spits out into another bay, where no person lives currently.

I have to assume my creek comes—searched for throughout this dry galaxy—from a hole in the ground. All right, *dilates from Earth's deep diaphragm*. But how deep, & how far into the forest? & why? Weeks spent bushwhacking, head low, the fevered search for source. *Why do you care so much*, someone wants to know? *You already know where it ends up. I've been washing in it*, I respond. I've soaked in its sun-heated drench. Kept my garden alive with it. *I've been drinking this water unfiltered for eighteen years!*

When I was young, I sang back to it.

# LOST WATERFALLS

**Steven Heighton**

> *For the strangled impulse there is no redemption*
> —Patrick Kavanagh

There was a waterfall, mapped in the founding
survey, two hundred years ago and lost,
eroded—something—so no later crew,
miner, or bushwalker has seen a thing.

                                        The river
it should have ruptured is still there, unspooling
where it ought to, out of the Burnt Hills down through timber
east of the Perth Road, chattering with chipped
fossils, flint-shards sparked by eels, then pooling
in a colonnade of cedars where the lost
falls should be exploding, still.

Went looking for you, what I thought was you.
A skirling of wind in the skymost branches
and peering round me for the radiant detonation,
vapours pulsing up from the sinkpool, I seem
to see the chalk-white shock of it—a cliffslide
through the cedars' warped, ashen balusters—
almost feeling the mist of this vision
condensed to a strange dew's
trickle down my face.

Wind dwindles then, dies, and that ghost-foam
flickers, the cataract-roar ebbs to the dodder
of a stone-bald, greying, oblivious river,
and I go.

Where have you got to? Gone to. Two hundred years,
the path healed over, the cedars deadfallen
or deeper in the sky, the mapmakers
deeper in the ground.

                    *There is a waterfall*, they lied,

afraid that love dries to a dotted line
on the map, that the river in time
slips underground, and  *This to prove*
*we were loved.* This whim
against what drifts to dark.

*We know, of course, it will not be found.*

# GROUNDWATER 2

**Maureen Scott Harris**


a contradiction in terms

ground joined to water
a kind of marriage—

    (isn't that mud?)

*water held in soil or rock,*
*especially that*
       *below*
*the water table*

    (a table made of water—
      how would it stand?)

groundwater is *held*

  beneath the water table
     hiding
       humming

    (listening to the grown-ups talk)

held under, held below
held by soil, held by rock

    (a mighty embrace)

yet is not still
or stagnant

he/she/it
     (gender is uncertain)
does not hurry
will not stop

(single
     minded)

penetrating

groundwater seeps
at a glacial pace
inching through voids

between grains of soil
pores in rock

    (rock solid)   (not)

when pressured flows up
tends down when partnered with gravity

like a hiker seeks and finds
the easiest—or only—way through

       For the sake of this poem
       let us call groundwater *she*
       confounding stereotypical expectations

       Reader, allow me to present
       the lovely groundwater

       (ravishing, indomitable)

       consider her constancy
       her full knowledge
       and embrace
       of the lay of the land

# TILTED SOUTH

**Al Rempel**

it's not until I stand around
with nothing to do maybe it's
Sunday in the dry creek bed
and I'm looking down
at all these rocks coated black
with dead algae & some stones
cracked open like clams
green & granite & red
and basaltic blue I don't know
where they came from

I look both ways up & down
see the land is tilted
everything sliding off
south to the ocean & maybe
these rocks remember
when winter locks them in
the ancient scrape of ice
that brought them here
and the lake that stayed awhile

they don't forget like we do
in the dead air of winter
all that water & what it says
when spring shucks off
layers of snow & ice
sheds the cold the sky
a thick blue above
a faint reminder

and then there's me
standing on these stones
with nothing much to do
looking north & looking south
and getting smaller
looking south
and getting
smaller

# American Bullfrog

**Dan MacIsaac**

Braggadocio
gonging over
the waterhole

Big-mouth
riotously drunk
on a jug-o'-rum

Yellow throat
ballooning to
a sun in a sack

Lout voluptuously
legged and
rudely tongued

Ill-bred from
a jellied throng
of zillions

Boaster infesting
westward to gorge
at a fetid trough

Bolting down
morphed slowpokes
and pipsqueaks

Raunchy cannibal
oafish home invader
engrossed by gluttony

In your drenched squat
you gloat
and gulp

In your lewd gob
any fair thing
is foul game

# Camping in the Time of Particulates

**Kevin Spenst**

From a bed, itchy eyes, then headlines, a cellphone with the same, a door, a back-pack, crows, ferns, boulders, a trail through the wilderness, dream-props waiting in the wings. You close your sweat-salted eyes to sleep. Consciousness remains a bulb soon dimmed, soon broken into shards and a sprawling filament whispers:

Ghosts of trees are haunting the sky, flying down with keepsakes.

When you dream, you enter a bed like a door, you walk down a hallway littered with branches and blades of orange, your backpack scratches at you, then bursts into coughing birds, a stepped on fern crunches to newsprint of 600 burning, the trail through the forest moves like an escalator while trees light up in neon and then shatter into small landslides.

Ghosts of trees are taking down the sky, bringing its breathlessness into our lungs.

When you wake in the dawn-warmed tent, your eyes open to the sun through the grey nylon and orange tarp. You close your eyes and the unseen sides of objects snap as if shadows were mousetraps. Something scurries outside. When you unzip the morning, you welcome a murmuration of browns and greens. You step into the role of object in the mind of the watershed. You breathe deep and listen, imagine your shadow in ashes.

# Two O'clock Creek

**Bruce Hunter**

All that summer couldn't understand
in the morning as we drove through
dry boulder wash, the matter-of-fact sign nailed
on a creekside spruce:
TWO O'CLOCK CREEK
—and no water anywhere.

Me twelve with Uncle John on patrol
in the forestry truck.
Him hungover and with that temper,
you didn't push the obvious.

But that sign taunted me.
As first ranger in the district
he named things factually like an explorer:
Abraham flats after a Stony chief
The map men kept that one,
thinking it Biblical and it was, in a way.

But each afternoon, driving back, sure enough
at two o'clock, there was a creek
roaring cold under the wheels.

Finally, a week before school and the city, I asked,
a prairie boy baffled by the magic of water
appearing anywhere, and on time.
John smirks, swings the Ford
into the ditch and around,
a madman on his way to a holy place.

I hang on as we climb, boulders boil in the fenders.
Double-clutching down into first
onto a horsetrail, then straight up on foot,
a pika whistling at us. Beginning to wish
I hadn't asked about that sign.

Over the alpine meadows
a plateau where mountain sheep startle
at the two of us covered in dust.
He draws his pipe across the crowfoot of a glacier
tipped from the distant sky, a white glory
scooped into the sunslope
in a sheltered cowl of rock.
John points to a green waterfall
spilling over the lip.

Here sky meets land
and water is hard as rock this high
and liquid ice to the tongue and our aching feet.
Where all the rivers begin,
the Whitegoat, the Bighorn
after the sheep behind us.
Headwaters of the upper Saskatchewan
I knew from schoolroom maps,
coursing down to Hudson Bay
with canoes full of coureur de bois.

Below us, blonde grass riffles on Kootenay Plains,
clouds jam the chute the weather comes through
where the Kootenay descended to barter the Cree.
Up here the wind howls cold.

And I saw how a few hours of daylight
warms the ice to a trickle that becomes a torrent
in the glacier's pit. The mystery of rivers
is that they come from somewhere
between earth and sky.
wrung by the sun from clouds and wind.

But when night comes, Two O'clock Creek sleeps,
the waterfall waits frozen, and all the years
since I learned how rivers are made,
this is the place I come to in my dreams
between the highest point of land and the sky,
so I can drink from the clouds.

# Our Own Lemon Creek

**Daniela Elza**

the road keeps narrowing

and we have this truck      full of jet fuel
to deliver.

and our road        it keeps narrowing
and the tyres slip and                 slip until

we flip             this life   into the river.

downstream
                —the water—      —murky—      —opaque—
white            with what can power the steel bird of

                                                a marriage.

silver                with the bellies of dead fish
                            the orders for evacuation.

                the air
—*don't breathe*—
          thick with poisons and
                                evaporation.

          upstream   I find brief refuge
      plagued by the repercussions
the ruined lives.

—paralyzed—
                —afraid— if I move

something might throw a spark—
start a fire—                          blow up—
what's left of             our fuselage.

# Godsend

**Ulrike Narwani**

> *I will walk barefoot—and in my shadow dusts*
> *of the shadows of lost things / quiver and shake.*
> —M. Travis Lane, "I Have Put On Mourning"

i

Seismic wave, unseen. Ocean doubled,
barreling down. Warning signs misread:
A sudden drawback of water, seabed exposed,
the flop and gasp of glistening fish
to be gathered in baskets by children.
Abundance, hailed godsend. No trumpet blast,
only deceptive reversal. Nature's
incubus pullback. Child into womb,
bird into egg, tree into seed. Razed trust.
*I will walk barefoot—and in my shadow dusts*

ii

*quiver and shake.* Heat wave, seismic.
Grasses rattle seed alert. Glaciers exhale
into ocean. Land, all Earth, bereft bears down.
We are left in receding swells, wear
widow's weeds, jingle beggar's bells. Scorched
the marrow of our days, parched the zings
of abundance in our throats. Desperate, we search
in deepest wells for tadpole, buds of tail and legs,
for prints in soft wet mud, hope's sure small springs
*in the shadows of lost things.*

# Dull Thuds over Waabiishkiigo Gchigami

**D.A. Lockhart**

Inland, on this three part island let it
resonate. Through summer night darkness
these dull, distant thunderbirds claps are

reminders rolling off stirred-up lake-effect spirits
that even distant storms find their ways to glacial
land upturned and shallow. Steady as nightfall

come to this limestone gouge, torrential
skies cloaking distant portions of Neutral Sea
inland, in this farmhouse, we may doubt glacial

ancestors in this bathtub sea, this night sky free
of the pathways left by stars, redolent grandmother
of a moon. The fear of trying one with the sea.

Here rattles a middle island farmer soul. Other
than fear or love he wanders between rooms
of this farmhouse, coaxed by light of grandmother.

Outside, clouds are broken and light casts
blooms of saturated moon light and we
watch on this three-part island. Listen well,
to these dull, distant claps of thunderbirds.

# Hesitating Once to Feel Glory

**Maleea Acker**

Sometimes I think we can see
the world before it began,
and that's what makes us
so sad. Before the world began

there were swallows flying
across a lakeside field
as the sun allowed the trees to shade it.
There were leaves fallen

during dry seasons that made
a golden road. And there was
silver and stone and clover,
and a man on horseback

with a dog with no tail
that loped across the field
in a lazy semi-crescent as though
drawing the orbit of a small moon.

There was a burro
on a ten foot length of rope
stomping a dust patch in the earth.
And there were pelicans

with injured wings handfed
by a waiter and so many willows –
so many! growing by the water's edge.
There was the clink of bottles

before the world began
and so its sound still
makes us melancholy
the way ice can, booming

on a river in spring
or tilling a glass in a woman's hand.
Stones, too, uncovered from earth
pockmarked with clam houses,

and also clams. Pianos, there were
pianos too, their cascade made us
restless, they could not offer
more nuance than the half note.

Things kept coming
before the world began, and stacked
and tumbled over themselves
in drifts like snow,

insensible. The world
before the world was annotated,
expansive, all the stones
the boys could throw

never hesitating once to feel
glory, to feel jealousy,
boredom, and the nostalgia
the grass feels as it clambers

above itself, and loses
its former lives in the clean,
disintegrating thatch
and dust and clay.

The sadness of the alternate
armed rower, who walked his boat
to shore! The sadness of the far shore
and the thud of a foot against a ball,

the bent hook of wire hanging
from a tree's lost branch stub,
the question in the ibis' voice
the sudden flash of a red bird

like a compass of ink in the brush.
Before the world began
there were bells that never
rang the correct time, and wings

and spheres of sad eggs in water.
The burrow walked his circle
and the carpenter never saw
his children further

than 6th grade. He never
painted his room yellow or cooked
on anything but a burner
on a board. And the neighbour,

after the party, she never
gave the plate back though
she said she would,
she always said she would.

# WARREN'S LANDING

## David Yerex Williamson

*for Moshum*

between a Red Rose cardboard
tea box of lead net
weights a jam jar
with four worn sewing awls
sits a china blue teacup
four black bear teeth
yellowing in the bottom

your fish shack
tells
a library
I cannot read

post trippers
long passed
dams awakening their souls
water beats forward a rhythm

between ribs
of an upturned yawl
you mended nets on the rock
past regaining shape

wind swept white caps sway
the river changing colours
the hydro lines buzz
over eroding shores
eight mile channel eats
the Nelson River

tired spring
your daughter sips
old afternoon wood smoke tea
canned milk memory dips into surface

returning this fisher
to shore
small hands keep safe
the knots you tied by water

from watershed to watershed
a beaver
follows the path

**Terry Ann Carter,**
after reading "Working with Beavers to Restore Watersheds"

# III. Grief

Denial ain't just a river in Egypt. —**Mark Twain**

Water is being depleted many, many times faster than nature can replenish it.
Unlimited growth assumes unlimited resources, and this is the genesis of Ecocide.
Do not listen to those who say there is nothing you can do
to the very real and large social and environmental issues of our time.
—**Maude Barlow**

Some time when the river is ice ask me
mistakes I have made. Ask me whether
what I have done is my life.
—**William Stafford**

# Russell Creek

**Dominique Russell**

> *Russell Creek is probably the most lost stream around*
> *Lost Rivers (Toronto)*

I've worn a groove
grieving a cousin, a brother, a father

A friend, hit by a truck,
friends, hit by sorrow—

Grief, I know you.
        You're the heart's goon

tearing wildly at clothes,
punching in the gut

you're hope that hooks
with brass-knuckled fact.

                        But this,
rising now, like a wall of water?

Did I love dragonflies, salamanders
duskywings, lady beetles?

Or even notice wild angelica,
bleeding hearts, milkweed?

I hated skinks and garter snakes
        I chose to live in a patchwork of cement.

And yet here I am on my knees again
while my children rescue worms

I listen for something moving
something buried that could rise.

# ANTHROPOCENE

**Arleen Paré**

How fathom water   watersheds   in this Anthropocene
sweet water clear water potable
or unpotable   translucent or murk
what threatens the transparent abundance   old news
toxins corporations deforestation   how fathom deforestation

last week city workers limbed the old willow
in the park near my house
last week   the day before the saws started their racketing noise
we watched the tree swing its long-fingered leaves in the wind
morning shadows and light sifting through to the grass
they removed its sweet weeping boughs
bared its trunk
mocked its grand sweep
beheaded the tree
then cut it down to the ground
each perfect round broad as a table

there are three million people in refugee camps
we are well into the sixth mass extinction
news enough

the first mass extinction left only 14% of the planet's species
the second removed 75   the third left only 4
millions of years have passed
no evidence remains
Devonian libraries   Triassic willows   watersheds
poems or refugee camps

one tree   how much I miss that one tree   that willow
whose roots still lace the water under the grass
grazing the river that runs under the park
runs under my house

## EXCERPT FROM *MAGNETIC NORTH: SEA VOYAGE TO SVALBARD*
**Jenna Butler**

4.

Mid June, and the boreal kindles like tallow.

No toxins across the water; here, one Players on the frontage grass and everything goes up, black spruce rickety with gum.

Each summer a little longer, a little hotter, and still the quads idling out in the muskeg, stink of gas in the deep woods. Used to be fork lightning, now it's Friday night bush parties, chainsaw sparks. I come home from water and ice to a forest spitting resin like midsummer rain. We watch the news, the wind. There's not enough water in Svalbard to put this forest out if it burns.

5.

Peat fires know to go underground, run out along the roots. A whole stand burning slowly from beneath.

Our first winter on the land, we lit a bonfire in a space of cleared ground to keep warm. Diamond willow, balsam poplar; everything we felled went into the flames, a long, slow burn. Potatoes in the coals and they would roast all day, pried from charred skins at twilight as the deep cold came down.

We learned that fire in the north is subterrain, that even the snow refused our circle, its heap of ash. Dug out the ground a week later and it was hot enough that you couldn't hold the soil without gloves. It smelt of roots and hair, a living, feral scent. Those are the fires you learn to fear, the ground going out from under your feet in an instant. Nothing left but cinders grasshoppering into the dark.

# Chernobyl Evacuee's Lament, Kopachi Village

**Ilona Martonfi**

When zinnias are blooming
we set a table with embroidered cloth
tend to our ancestors' gravestones
toast with plum brandy

in the old cemetery,
here is Vladimir and Aleksandr

don't touch anything. Don't stray,
stay on concrete and asphalt
shrouded reactor 4
90 kilometers from Kiev
that morning
without a warning
clouds raining down isotopes

along woodland and peat bogs
blueberry season
laced with caesium, strontium
Pripyat River watershed

buried village of Kopachi

nesting black storks.
Radioactive wolves.
How can you forget it?

Windows broken. Doors.
Nothing was left.

Garden untended.
Apple tree. Pear tree.

# WHETHER REPORT

**Marion Quednau**

*Weather—The state of the atmosphere with respect to wind, temperatures, etc. Changes or vicissitudes in one's lot or fortunes.*

*Whether—used to introduce a single alternative, the other implied or understood …*

A forked spring, undecided—
winter, in its cold, precious delay
                            not yet delivered,
the fields white-staged with flailing trumpeter swan
                            never flown south—
trees still dropping last year's bright leaves,
a slim hope for blossoms
                hanging on a few reckless buds.
Summer, as recompense,
                as wracked and surprising—
a rilling of water on every green surface,
                then scathing drought, coral fires in the hills.


The she-dog, in the seasons' stale commotion,
mated with her brother,
                her offspring a twosome:
one a black-faced shivering pup, fitful and howling,
        the other an innocence
with curious webbed feet and wings,
                that would not live to morning.
A dawn then that seemed like day's end,
                dark birds dropping lifeless from the sky
in their delicate tizzy of murmuration—
a high wind and squalling,
                            lightning striking twice
the second-to-highest ridge—two horses
                kept both for pleasure and for kindness
lying prone in the charged air.

Those dwelling by the river's divide
                              saw the steep air
grow ice-white with shattering hail,
            abandoned
their safe-gated, panic-roomed houses
            with a thirsting, beneath the slant sky,
for omens—
                              some even danced.
It was all happening at once
                              and already ended—
with only faint-whispered recall
                  of former harvest or harmony.


                  There would be softer hours,
landscape grown to sage and rust,
                  a stillness without amaze;
those caught in the openness
swore they saw walking fishes, and a pride
                  of dark caracals, long extinct,
pacing among the handsome dead—
spoke of the awkward joy
            *in having been found*—
knew two unscribed languages in their sleep,
the shrill want of themselves
                              and the thrilling of the earth's tongue,
long exhausted, and still, in its syllables
            of broken rock and spun water, so pure—
its soft-spoken moss and greens,
                  dark nestlings of decay,
laid open
      to the ongoing human ruckus
for bigger and best, the hard-won moon
                  gaping toward ruin.

# IF THIS WAS THE EUPHRATES

**Emily Wall**

A dead barn swallow
floats by this morning along
the green throat of the river.

How can we not believe
in Eden? With all of this
watershed at our feet?

We have scraped and dulled
the edges of it—a metal warehouse
a cement plant, a parking lot.

We have declared our
intention to live here, our
ownership over grass and light—

and then we love it
a little less.  But if we lie
down on the dock tonight

our faces inches from
this estuary, we can see
it as a barn swallow does—

a plate heaped with grasses,
dragonflies, crickets, moths.
It fills our whole sight

and begins to feel like a familiar
river we could return on,
our bones light as breath

our bellies full of wings.
Look, somewhere in this grass
there's a gate.  No security guard

or flaming angel.  Just one flashing
silver tail, one feathered foot.
One deep swallow of clean.

# Sleeping with the River

**Dorothy Field**

There was a pond where winter people used to skate
and from the pond a creek, its name
forgotten.
        I sleep over that stream, rocked in the land's carrying basket,
               its woven edge the crest of the hills, my bed a boat beached
                   on sand damp with her roll and tidal reach.
A century ago, Haida and Tlingit edged up to Fort Victoria,
camped beside Rock Bay, traded fish and clams
for guns and knives. Settlers polluted the creek – bloody mattresses,
broken plates, coal gas sludge. City fathers disappeared
        her waters deep in brick culverts.
                       Still she courses, her web of rivulets
              pour themselves into the Gorge, mix with ocean salt.
          Still she heaves the built cityscape: floods basements, burbles up
     through pavement, trickles neighbourhood streets: Grant, Blanshard, Queens.
Finlayson Falls, her rocky waterfall, long blasted away.
        Lost and almost gone, her waters
          still pour into Rock Bay, sing to no-longer cedars
                 paved-over eel grass.
My ear to manhole covers, I listen
for her sparkle.

Dream the creek: that I may see her
brought back to the light of day,
sit on her banks, count dragonflies and tadpoles
        while kids dabble her shallows
              and coho swim upstream to spawn.
Dream my feet trodding her course,
        the hop of frog, the wood duck's sweep,
        the plash of returning salmon:
           the stream renewed to living wildness.

Bend to her dialect.
   O Earth, if I forget this creek – and all our waters,
        let my tongue stick to the roof of my mouth
        my hand forget to stroke my beloved
            my parched lips dumb as the river's
            silenced song.

# Yellow Deck Chair, Black-Legged Ticks, Cracked Glass in Wood Frames

**Lorri Neilsen Glenn**

Do I dare walk the path to the water? Late spring
grasses pulsate with ectoparasitic danger and I've
been there, the aches, the weeks on drugs. From

the safety of the road, I peer into the bower where
deer rise early each morning. I wait at dusk for their
dun bodies to ribbon a path across the yard.

A madman has taken a scythe to the world. I've taken
to craning in the dark for stars: is cold hope enough?
Before dawn, I will hear Jason's boat cross the bay.

My aunt woke late on her 103rd birthday. I never sleep
in, she says. Every day shorter. Every week, my sister
drives her husband with his dying heart to the clinic.

How do days rush by like fluttering wings? Back at
the house, a flatbed truck, its door open. A wiry man
scuttles around the corner, a two-toothed grin, eyes lit

with, what? this warm spring day, the ease of the job?
He once shovelled sewage in August heat to repair
the septic. Today, it was a pipe. He salutes and is gone.

Inside, I read Levertov, Bukowski. His words rankle:
"writing has to come out like hot turds the morning
after a good beer drunk." Oh Chuck. I must be a

prig, a pearl-clutcher. Does it all, finally, come to
sewage? Are the tropes I draw on naïve, callow?
I am adept at the weave, the warp and woof of rage

and I dread despair. Could I, like Wright, break into
blossom? Learn to find beauty in devastation, in
waste? I'm no Burtynsky—opened, raw, I am flayed

by it all: oceans gagging on garbage, deformed fish,
poison running in Northern rivers. Mountain ice
thawing by the year and here, by the shore, a spring

silence in the trees like a child's funeral. Humans are
1/10,000 of earth's biomass: how's that working?
Reader, I know you want sense here. I could say we

have embraced the wrong gods, not loved enough
—not the waxwings at the feeder nor what stirs
under the moon. But it's all been said: wisdom is

a bad mixtape; philosophy a bumper sticker. For
now, I'll wait in the yellow deck chair for the sun
to disappear and the horizon turn every shade

of red, even blood, until I hear the ocean breathe.
The deer are alert by the barn: I don't move or
meet their gaze: something around here ought to

feel safe. But tires snap on gravel, voices rise
and the deer bolt. Pickers load the broken windows,
leave dust in their wake. I pull the word *gloaming*

from the still air. Dark ticks down, the neighbour's
hound bays, a crane glides over water and stars reveal
themselves. I love this world. I mourn it every day.

# I Could Simply Give In

**D.C. Reid**

It is morning and I am kneeling
in the river that trembles my hand.

There is flesh in this morning,
the fragile of sockeye, living on

in winter where they should not live.
There is the beat of a hidden heart,

and the river gives and takes a life.
My hands grow ghostly

at the ends of my arms.
The flesh in them will not end today.

The blue-green knowledge
of water is: Sitka, cedar and sedge.

As though a coastline makes a difference.
A ragged place of feet in boots and laces

come free. Only the legs keep moving,
scattering salmon that should not be.

Their purpose is as ours: to make
an acquaintance and break

in water the colour of thought.
I could simply give in to making life.

My feet, trembled into nothing,
run red rocks from the basement

of time. They know no other
purpose than striding the Taylor,

the Elk, the San Juan,
any source of knowledge

that is passed to the tree
after it is passed through me.

# THE LAST LAKE STURGEON

**Christine Schrum**

They outlived the dinosaurs
but we've brought them to the brink
of extinction. In Lake Superior
the silver bellies of sturgeon swell
with minuscule plastic beads
because we wanted
blackberry sugar body wash,
acne exfoliator, 3D white teeth,
a little skin glitter
to make our limbs shimmer
like sunlight on fish scales.

It's not a sexy word, is it?
*Sturgeon.* Squelching syllables
suitable for one who sucks
snails and crustaceans from soft mud
with a syphon-like mouth.
But have you ever seen
the crocodile-plated knight
of the Great Lakes, the tail-walker
who playfully jumps and twirls
like a dolphin, who can swim
on his knobby back just like you and me?
Did you know this shark-finned fish
can live longer than a century,
or that his ancestors tickled the toes
of the thirsty Tyrannosaurus?

We may yet save the Spirit Bear,
the orca, the snow leopard,
the eminently photogenic
giant panda. But the lowly
bottom feeders will be the first
to go—those who are not cute, cuddly,
or flashy enough for an IMAX.

That which we deem ugly
we overfish, overlook, overrun.
Who will mourn
the last gasping sturgeon,
deep in the barren Great Lakes?

# Planetary Hubris

**Kirsten Pendreigh**

There's a scientist on the radio talking turbines in the Arctic:
if we install ten million, we could cool things down.

They're cloud seeding in Tasmania to make it rain.
In Tahoe, to make it snow.

Silver iodide rockets shoot into the skies.
No one's sure it works, but Thailand has a Bureau of Royal Rainmaking.

Mitigation. Adaptation.
Buzzwords for our warming world.

The Geritol solution: massive ocean dumps of iron
to fertilize the plants that suck up $CO_2$

or stratospheric sulphur shots, to boost the Earth's albedo,
so less sun gets through.

Perfectly safe? Probably, say scientists at MIT.
Do they remember Starfish Prime—the high-altitude H-Bomb

that stunned its own creators with its force.
I once hiked in White Sands, site of the first nuclear detonation.

Was almost bitten by a rattlesnake.
It reared its head up, out of nowhere.

# FALLING SCENE

**Jeremy Pataky**

The falling snow is plasticine.
It glibly mocks the Pleistocene.
The planet's just a magazine.

The Anthropocene is hip
to irony and tolerates sincerity,
berates vulgarity but takes it,
takes it, swallows it
then gargles
with bottled water,
      warm "glacier" water,
            vintage water, Nestle water
      muni water, ag water, pipeline water

            Flint water,
      homemade water cooked from slabs of lake ice.

Prepper water in crawlspace jugs or bathtubs.

          The Anthroposcenesters were finished
      with the Anthropocene's budding billions,
humans abuzz by dry hotsand beaches,
interminable white noise of waves beneath gull calls,
authentic nostalgias, memories, even,
all underlined with a long wall
bought by Mexico.

    *Fukushima water and DAPL water*

Only the sound of a tweet
will evoke the present scene,
tense with its
*it's-not-too-lates*
where children—*just playing*—
stuff siphons into schools' throats,
into banks' throats, into
automobiles' and jets'

throats, their parents
neigh and singing worthy praises
to the mutilated world,
stopping on their ways for Syrup of Ipecac
and Molotov cocktails, holiday cordials
and grandfathers' firearms.

*Firewater. Filtered water.*

Today, the uprising's downfall ticked up a point on the exchange.
Every scene so far's been action of one sort or another.

We are not the species going extinct here,
here in the Resistance,
here in our resilience,
here in the schitzocene.

*Holy water. Sewer water.*

Equity is the bodily vulnerability
it turns out we all have in common
under the right circumstances.

*What is loneliness, anyway, they would ask,*
        *if you're at least safe from physical attack?*

                *Dunk tank water. Sunny day flood water.*
                        *Waterboarding water.*

Our differences map
who harms and receives harm,

in a nation always a harem for harmers
a field plowed under by powers

pitting peoples against the people
bedwetters prone and prison-tied in beds

homeless, landless, soilless, soiled, souled.

        *Sold.*

# Lost Lake

**Adelia MacWilliam**

> *after a line by Gary Snyder*
> *For M.G.*

Well, it's a retro Bar and Grill now in Seattle,
where the light is a woman ducking into a doorway
between the *calligraphy of cars* on Capitol Hill, as seen from
above by a hawk, not far from the Elliot Bay bookstore.
Yes, it's a Bar and Grill open twenty-four seven now,
where steelhead trout ghost by damply unseen
behind the whiskey and gin, and the cougar
on the shelf above the window has a plastic grin.

Please wait to be seated in Lost Lake,
where all the wildernesses meet. You can look for Yoko Ono's
tiny yes on the ceiling just visible through a magnifying glass.
Lao Tzu will be there wearing a baseball cap,
also saying yes, while Gary Snyder's *Mountains and Rivers Without End*
opens its pages
in a booth in the back, unanswered koans near the ketchup,
and the girls at the next table joke about last night's escapades
on the "D" train.

We'll meet in the back booth and you'll tell me the story
of your first meeting with the Dalai Lama,
how your mala broke, beads peppering the airport floor.
His Holiness helped you pick them up
and when you asked him what this meant,
he told you, "Scattered blessings."

# Exorcise

**Elee Kraljii Gardiner**

Deep in the cedars I bring ocean out onto my skin.
Splatters from the crown let everything wet,
puddling in the crotch of trees. Saturated
nurse logs spruce up with plump pads of moss.
The buds bleating pop music slide out of my ears
while mist settles amidst root systems.

On the trail I do not smile at men. Women have dogs,
we *hey* each other but the men, no:
they run importantly, tight-elbowed

in New Balance and shorts flaunting core
heat despite dipping degrees. They hate
waiting. I do not owe them a thing.

The radio in the car states a killer has been charged
with violating a 13-year-old girl's body and throwing it
in the bushes of a park. I don't owe men anything.
I pour rainwater out of my backpack,
the skies of Russia pool in the footwell.

On the bridge across the inlet truckspray
greys my vision. I drive blind, tires reading in Braille.
My thighs are plastered cold and my neck
sloughs its dried grit: the pinch dish
of Himalayan salt he keeps by the stove.

Bark filings sneak through my socks.
Bathwater raises my blood—particulates
of Baden Powell's colonialism—to the surface.

My salt sighs. I slide soap down my stomach as chainsaws eat
the trees next door, choking the air with splinters.

# Hydrophobia

**Aaron Kreuter**

A glass of water, half full or half empty. Your childhood bathtub, full of poison. A street of milk chocolate brown puddles after an overnight rainfall nobody saw nor heard, a minefield. A sun shower. A rainstorm. A torrential downpour. Tidal waves that heard what you said about them. All the murdered lakes back for horror-movie-style revenge. (Every toilet bowl you pass spooks you into recoil, a porcelain mouth of deranged fangs.) The lake and river systems you once spent happy summers paddling now magma burning with the shrieks of your loved ones. The thirst of a billion throats, heaving oceans of salty fear. Comets of ice slam into the atmosphere, firework into liquid death. You dream nightmares of each one of your hundred trillion cells, swampy nightclubs where every dancing body is a pedophile a murderer a childhood enemy who knows your sexual secrets, you wake up to discover the ice caps have melted your bed afloat on a sea of knives you scream and scream your thirst a stovetop burner levered full blast *water knows no boundaries* you scream *water has skin as soft as pudding as hard as toothache water has sense memory* you holler *from the first spark of 'huh, this is nice' to the last bureaucrat dumping the last load of poison into the last river—from salty womb to wet loam—water's been with us* you stop the roar of rising tides drowning you out the planet drowning you wish for two things one to swing a little further from the sun all the water sucked up into glorious skyscrapers of ice two to swing just a little closer close enough for it all to evaporate into steam to puff into space leaving everything dry, flopping, crusted. The water sloshes, slaps, spits, and you're finally parched enough to gulp liquid rock.

# By the Glass

**Rhona McAdam**

Free for the taking
through all my childhood,
crashing into glasses bouldered with ice,
poured thickly from the sides of plastic jugs,
the unremarked and neglected
sentry at the top of place settings,
sweating on formica,
seized to cure fits of coughing
or moments of spice, replenished
unasked and endlessly.

When the costly bottles came,
in thalassic greens and fluvial blues,
the taps still turned for the frugal,
and we got what we paid for,
tepid, swirling with mist, fragrant
with swamp, or sold for 10 p a glass
at a parsimonious caff in Cornwall.
We drank each chlorinated drop
and spared the tip.

In New Mexico restaurants,
cards propped on the tables
invited us to value even this, the stuff
of dishpans and swimming pools,
while all afternoon in the Hilton
the self-flushing toilets
thundered their copious refrain
in unoccupied stalls.

A friend has returned from Africa.
We sit on the beach in clothes the colour of sand,
watching clouds gather
on the undrinkable blue horizon.

# WATERSHED SONNET

**David Pimm**

Despite saline
        rain
that flushes the shallow
wetlands, grease, oil—viscous—
still pollute the fluid mix. Debris—
slag and silt—clogs the cattails,
those freshwatered fronds.
Each lacquered lash corrodes.
A blood moon occludes the view.
Overnight, murk seeps the bleak
face of the nearby crag: this rock-
stalk stye, alien growth, blush-red.
    Ruddied, my eyelid swells—my eyesight
    blurred by bloodied rust.

# WATER IS LIFE OR DEATH

**Dennis Saddleman**

Water it's calm
Water it's flowing
Water it's deep
Water it's cold
Water it's flooding
Water it's dripping
Water in my thoughts
At the sink, I watched the water coming out of the tap
At the sink, I watched the water going down the drain
Oh water! Water! I didn't know you
A long time ago, I was afraid of you, I was afraid of you
A long time ago someone, someone didn't like me
Someone was angry, someone threw me in the deep water
I didn't know how to swim, I didn't know how to swim
There was a splash, water was cold
Panic kicked in, I saw white bubbly water
No time to breathe, no time to breathe
I kicked my legs   I tried to stay afloat
I moved my arms frantically
I started sinking.  I sank like a rock
I blacked out   I blacked out  I blacked out
I came to someone was pushing on my chest, water came out of my mouth
Someone asked, are you okay?   I nodded my head yes
Someone stood up and he walked away
I never knew his name, I never saw him again
I wondered if he was an angel who saved my life
At the sink, I watched the water coming out of the tap
At the sink, I watched the water going down the drain
Oh water! Water! Who are you?
For long time, I've been drowning in own fears, I've been drowning
Throw a rock in the water, it will sink and you wondered if the rock drowned
Oh water! Water! Do not take me away  Water! Water! I'm just a boy
I do not want to drown with my boyhood
Big waves of water hit the shore   Big wave of water splashed the rocks  Big waves of
    water tried to catch me

I ran and ran and ran
I was afraid of the water, deep deep water
I was afraid of swimming pools, I was afraid of the creeks
I was afraid of the river near my home
I was afraid of the lakes, I was afraid
I was getting nowhere with my life, I didn't like this world of darkness
I didn't like this world of fear, I didn't belong here
I must take a big big breath, I must jump in the pool of courage
I must wash myself with trust
There she was, there she was   She was standing in the shallow water
They said, she walks with the ancestors
She had red hair   Her voice was gentle   She told me
Close your eyes   Close your eyes   Talk to yourself
Tell yourself, it's going to be okay
Touch the water   Touch the water   The Water wants to shake hands with you
The water wants to be your friend
It's okay! it's okay!   The water it's soft   The water it's gentle   The water it's our
    relative
I was floating on water, floating on water, I was doing the dog paddle, doing the dog
    paddle
At the sink, I watched the water coming out of the tap
At the sink, I watched the water going down the drain and I turned off the tap
Oh Water! Water!
You didn't have friends, your life was a struggle just like mine
You became sick and nobody cared
One night I looked up to the sky, I saw the big dipper
My grampa asked, do you know what's in the big dipper?  I said, No
My grampa said, Sacred Water    You tip the dipper in the sky and the sacred water
    will spill on Mother Earth
That's why every drop of water is sacred
You must protect the water, you must respect the water
Water is precious water is life, water is life

# High Water Mark

**Maureen Hynes**

We descend the steel stairs, look up to where the hurricane slid
her hand up the bridge's tower. Walk beneath the wavy
high water mark and remember that the river's always

been that deep. Join anglers, gulls and cormorants, each on a private
quest—absorb a sudden patience, the swerve of dragonflies,
trace pre-glacial watercourses, their stops and turns and signs.

*The land's a living thing,* said Bonnie Devine. In her mural
she painted the Great Lakes red—the continent's heart, its arteries
the rivers. *Water always in dispute, in dispute still.* Someone's

poisoned a tiny brook in this riverside park, turned it rust-red,
poured in an oily brine that floats atop—we could crouch
and light it like a long fuse. Beyond, midstream waders snap

and reel their fishing lines. Knotweed and nuthatches, trout lily
and thorns. On a sunlit log, a mourning cloak fans and folds her wings.
A corroded hubcap on the ground, mirror to a dried-out stump,

its rings cracked apart. We gather broken glass and bottle caps and
Styrofoam bits. Leave behind rusty runoff and swirling cream sludge,
juncos and flickers, the glittering river afternoon. Above us,
a man sings a Verdi aria, floats it over all of us from the bridge.

# Under Western Water: Returning to Work

**Richard Harrison**

My books stood by the water resting at their wooden shore,
    and they were patient and quiet and the water had stopped
        rising in my house and in the houses of all my neighbours.

The books reminded me of penguins waiting at the icy edge of the sea,
    none of them wants to be first in case there's a leopard seal
        under the surface.

Sooner or later (we've all seen the films), one of them falls—
    if it lives, the rest go in because it's safe,
        if it dies, the rest go in because the seal isn't hungry anymore.

Sometimes when I'm walking across a bridge,
        I feel that strange gravity that says, *Go on, you want to,*
    and when I think of all those books with their spines and their silence,
I feel the anger of parents who shout at children
    who don't get hit by cars even though they walked
        into the street without looking.

I say, *The water was right there*
    *and my books looked like they were standing on the shore,*
        and my friends, whose love you can measure in their listening,
    smile and say, *You're writing a poem, aren't you?*

More words is the answer to the fact that a book,
fallen into the water,
takes the same second between life and death
to be ruined by its own pages.

A piece of paper born to soak up all the meaning
that ink can give will take a drink from any water it's offered,
and then it will bloat, and relieve itself of everything it held.

Where I didn't save them,
    the books thickened so much with water
        they split their shelves.

—∞—

I moved around the flooded basement.
        Things drifted between the bookshelves
           and the submerged futon and the darkened warping boards
              of the piano that was slowly being destroyed.

Some of those things were cards we'd saved from all card-occasions:
birthday cards and anniversary cards, and congratulations and sickness
and every one of those cards was blank
because the card stock shed all its ink into the water
                       and all the meaning was let go.

So I read them as sympathy cards from the river, saying,
*Sorry. I couldn't have done anything else. I'm sorry.*

And I was not moving in the basement,
just standing, waiting for the ripples I had made to go still.

It's like that moment when the therapist asked,
        *How did you feel?* and I answered,
           *I was thinking about being small, about being nothing,*

and there I found the blank place in my mind
        that has winked open every so often ever since,
           even in the middle of the working day.

I'll be typing a letter,
        and I'll look away from the screen
           and look back and wonder what I was typing,
and who was waiting for me,
              but that's not where I was going.

—∞—

I was going was to tell you
        that sometimes the water itself just moved—
           it rose a little at one end of the room,
          like something tilted the house from below.

And there it was, the proof: I was standing in a tiny part
of a mass of water that connected
                    all the cities and towns and villages along the river,
                         water that spread over the city,

        remaking it,
        drawing a new topographical waterline all over it
                with everything below that line wounded.

I was in the body of a great silent beast,
            the landscape, and the waterway,
                    and the rain revealing itself at once
                            from behind civilization's enormous forgetting.

# Post-Concussion Syndrome, or; The Impacts of Protest

**Jackie Seidel**

December 4, 2015. Ghost River Watershed. Bow Valley. Alberta. Canada.

We tried.
And.
The children tried, with
    their bittersweetbitter signs
    *Save The Trees*
Our cold feet stamp the snow
But because.
Because rumbletrucks feller-bunchers bulldozer hard hats steel-toed boots F150 profit
Because.

It seems only right then. That
The December ice-ground slipped me and
Our crowns crashed together into this roughed up
Earth.

It seems only right then. That this extended hand to break the slipfall compels shoul-
der bones to fracture separating ligaments while the forest is cracked wide open in
a single night and fragments displaced concussing dizzy ear ringing too bright lights
my brain is now also a clearcut while the world spins on.

Welcomed by the soil now, we are.
We are both
Not right.
Together.

# BLUEBERRY CREEK

**Barbara Pelman**

> *What would the world be, once bereft*
> *Of wet and of wildness? Let them be left*
> *O let them be left, wildness and wet*
> *Long live the weeds and the wilderness yet.*
> —Gerard Manley Hopkins

Mornings we walked, with the dog
and a small grey fog of a cat, following the creek
to where it met the river, the Columbia,
and on its banks, our small red house.
Past salal and cottonwood, the creek
spoke its noisy spring language: water
over pebble, waterfalling down ledges, and the river
answered in its deep largo music.
The wide river, the noisy creek, the dog, the cat—

*What would the world be, once bereft*

of willow and alder, spring blooming of lupin
bluing the hillside, and down near the bank,
sedge grass and scrub. Our boots squelching
on riparian pathways, call of an owl
on the early morning wind. The creek widens
below the house, opens to the river,
so wide the far shore dims and fades.
And what would we have done, after office and traffic,
without the owl, the grasses, the sounds

*Of wet and of wildness? Let them be left*

though that was long ago and the house
has been razed or maybe renovated, and I live
in the city, where owls are rare and the wind
blows eerie through the telephone wires.
Creeks here are roped and tidied, their banks

not clustered with fern but walled with rock
or tucked under roads. No chance to wander
barefoot along the stream beds, balance
on boulders, hair tangled with willow branch—

*O let them be left, wildness and wet*

The bogs, the small creeks running,
the mountain streams crashing over rock
or trickling summerly, rainbow trout running
under lucent water, the salmon spawning
in the river, children racing the banks
so that they know, they will know, to bless the fish
in the rivers, the bear behind the trees,
the orca jumping in the Salish Sea, the water
they can still cup in their hands and drink from the holy streams—

*Long live the weeds and the wilderness yet.*

# EXCERPT FROM "THE LOST LAND"

**Murray Mann**

> *It is estimated by Triton Logging that*
> *there are 10 million cubic meters of timber*
> *underwater in the Ootsa Lake reservoir and*
> *eighty-five percent of that is over sixty feet in depth—*
> *the ideal depth for their starfish, they note—*
> *(a machine used to harvest timber underwater)*

Beneath these waters lie the silted remains of a land:
an old land, a forgotten land, the lakes no longer lakes
and the rivers no longer rivers. Whole forests, whole lakes

whole rivers lie buried beneath these corporate waters.
This land, buried under water and forgotten for sixty years:
sixty years of silt and sediment, in a dim light, a watery-cold dark light

deep waters; cold waters, not moving, not flowing
but drained in a slow awkward westward movement
through a man-made tunnel, through the coastal mountains.

This land, here
under these waters
now seems more like the land of the dead.

Yet I shall say the names. The old names.
The names of the lakes (and if there be spirits,
then let them help my work) for there was:

NATALKUZ
INTATA
OOTSA
SINCLAIR
TAHTSA
WHITESAIL
EUCHU
TETACHUCK
CHELASLIE

and EUTSUK alone survived—
silent voice of the past.

# Water Crossings

**Elena Johnson**

1.

| | |
|---|---|
| (The vast majority of) | the pipeline will be |
| (buried) | up to |
| | a metre underground. |
| | The only exceptions will be |
| (select) | water |
| (crossings) | where it is safer |
| (to run the pipeline) | above |
| (the water crossing) | . |

2.

| | |
|---|---|
| (Around) | small creeks |
| | beaver dams |
| (create dynamic) | wetland complexes |
| (of) | shallow water |
| | sedge marsh |
| (and) | willow swamp |
| (which are) | |
| (exceptionally) | |
| (important for) | wildlife. Marshes |
| (occur around) | lakes and |
| | streams, |
| (usually with) | horsetails |
| (and sedges,) | |
| (but also with) | |
| (stands of) | cattail, bulrush, and spikerush |
| (in the warmer) | |
| (parts of the zone) | . |

# You make me ache river with your—let me say it

**Catherine Owen**

You make me ache river with your—let me say it—beauty—& the way

they've tortured you—you fill with
creosote & cadmium—minus signs swim
in your shallows—alongside your shores,
dump trucks line up like taxis, each allotted
two metal handfuls—

geese veeing through the plume from Lafarge—this is why I came to Canada,

you hear her say—all those booms
in the river—she thought it was
fascinating, the best part of geography—no,
nothing more romantic than the death of trees,
cells upon cells of them leashed—yarded

& those adorable little tugs called Storm Surf, called Old School—yes you make me

ache, river, because I cannot
save you & who am I to save
anyone—I couldn't even save
him, though he wrote—before
the last hit—that I was his

*dark angel of mercy*—yuck! —there is no subservient hope in these waters, beloved—

the crows scatter back from the woods,
trucks pull into the lot & it follows
its own fate—the river—burning again
with sunrise—as if it had never

known grief.

# -40°C

**Eleonore Schönmaier**

She opens the door. A few pairs
of shoes all patched

with duct-tape. The kitchen
table covered with a Christmas

cloth, and there is one
place setting. The lower half

of the walls are crumbling
from rot. On the bookshelf:

Goethe, T.S. Eliot, Dostoyevsky. The brown
water stain on the bedroom ceiling

is as large as the room. She sits
at the piano and begins

to play. The black
bathroom mold creates its own

art gallery. On the turn-table:
Beethoven's violin concerto.

She turns up the heat: the house
will be warm for the first

time in fifty years. Father.
Are there not many versions

of warmth and wealth? At the funeral
the last man to leave says, "He was

the original
environmentalist." He wore

out his few possessions
at the same rate as his life: slowly

and with no replacements parts.
At the end his sweater in shreds

as he lay on the shoulder
of the winter ice road

his hands still gripping
the bike handlebars.

His basement
full of bushels

of garden potatoes, homemade
raspberry and blueberry

jam. And in the garage
the freezer (not plugged in) full

of beets, beans, pickerel
and carrots. Five bicycles

hang on their racks, and the walls
are lined with garden

tools, cross-country
skis. What more

does one need than this?
The church was packed

with his friends. She keeps the fishing
reel and sets it on her desk

with its two black
arms, its silver head:

the plastic line ready
to unspool into a small

lake with enough
fish for all her needs.

# KUS-KUS-SUM

**Lorin Medley**

*1. Field's sawmill*

A burial site with ghost bodies
                                    on platforms  in trees
retaining walls at the river's edge

log booms float in the memory water
past Hollyhock Marsh    upriver  to the mill

in the lumber yard   forklifts  front end loaders
Ross and Marty on the green chain        yellow cedar 4 x 4s

*Love it or hate it*   concedes the waitress at The Old House
Monte Cristo above the ambient bandsaw
whose bite and zing carries across the river

downstream                    bones in the midden
        winged chevron of fish traps
                        storied tumble of salmon

estuary    the tidal mouth of a large river
mud mouth        salt chew


*2. We the marsh*

                        Lost fish  we
heart and flank the watershed
pave and unpave paradise        dismantle
the wall    install it in a Ken Gerberick forest
with old cars  rust    and moss        we oil and eagle
hawk and plover    crab and  flounder    loon and grebe
we  *other* the marsh

picked off by seals at the killing wall      salmon
diminish      the mill closes   but
salt marsh fills in    toxins in the surface clay

orphans of the living sediment  we face the stars
water eyed      hunger for the cold sea
to toss and return the story
        begin again

with Pacific cinquefoil    tufted hairgrass
herring roe in the eel grass    camas and shooting stars

begin again with a village        and a name

# Peace Country

**Pamela Porter**

*R.I.P Peace River Canyon*

I.

Nearly May and snow
holding to the north side of the barn, grass
sodden with melt, her boots soaked through.
And beside, an open shed tumbling out grey wood,
and the drowning-pond's treacherous ice
covering its own darkness, below the vista
of budded birch and fir, the barn windows
spilling their damp breath.

In the distance the coal cars humped down the tracks
where the land was slashed and sutured, a wound
that scared her more because she knew it was her life
refusing to heal. She thought finding him would be enough,
enough to declare she was his daughter, meaning acceptance,
a fact. But there was more she'd have to prove, and lay
on her back in the hay, inhaling its hay smell
while swallows mudded the walls of their houses
in expectation for the life to break open,
the small hard beaks' relentless tapping.

And she reckoned he thought in lamplit evenings how
a daughter was burden, a burlapped load. In a broken
piece of mirror she saw a torn girl,
a mustang without brand. *To belong*—
the age in him a solid thing, like wood, his years
heavy enough to lean on, but it might turn out
he'd drop her out back like an old sofa,
a life instantly simpler for the act, she pondered
while her fingers combed her hair like a mane.
She had chosen him, and waited.

A heart's all creaking doors and peeling paint
and rusted latches, windows staring in stunned wonder.
She'd do what she could—forgive herself her poverty
and knock, quiet, on his rattling door, listen
for his breathing inside, hands in his pockets,
and behind her the pond like a moon fallen to the grass
and spring working its slow determined will.


II.


As the eagle pair carried twigs and fur to the blown top
of the pine, and rain turned to snow and back again
stitching grey sky to ground, the old man and girl
ate in silence his spare cooking, the hearth fire
spitting out its opinions, the slow earth hardening
only as the sun allowed.

The girl made up her mind she'd track the horse
he'd let go wild and once over supper he spoke enough
to say she could have it if she could catch it and so
spent her first spring in that place, following the horse
she guessed had a few years still in him, and thought
the same about the old man.

A horse who trusted no one and a man with so many
wounds in him, she knew when she lay in bed
watching moonlight pour over the splintered sill,
no girl could stitch them all shut. And the horse
she also approached in silence, how it grazed the field
with an eye on her while she inched closer by the day.

The old man too kept his good eye on her, a serious face
she'd brought from the no-place she came from. Every dawn
she walked among wormwood and ash in search of the horse,
a dun with raven mane, and knelt in the lengthening grass
knotting a rope halter from scrap as robins tugged at the soil
and fireweed blossomed out of stone.

When not with the horse she was in the corral nailing
the fallen boards back. The evening she waded halfway
into the creek, slipped the halter over the muzzle
and led the horse home, he saw her coming, the reflection
of sky and cloud covering his face in the window,
how she stood on a rail to mount, the flesh rippling

beneath her hands, the dark stripe down its spine
between her legs. Everywhere in that country, wild rose
tangled itself in barbed wire, and down where the creek
met the river, the canyon spilled its secrets.
She knew nothing else in that moment
but the great horse heart beating through its skin

and the first hesitant steps until she passed
his cracked hands laced together over the fence,
some lost life reborn in his face. And felt inside him
a broken place mending over, while the moon
started up the pine, the three of them together
in the late June light, breathing the untamed air.


III.

The girl knew she would stay until she buried the old man,
and then maybe she'd move on, she thought, riding the horse
across the fields, dried flowers, the land asleep, how she
could hear the hills' wild breathing in the afternoon, the haze,
smoke in the air from fires up north. The horse snorted
and shook its head, spilling flies she rode through,
one hand on reins braided from baling twine,

and with the other traced the line of black that ran down
its spine. She'd stay to mend the curtains, brush cobwebs
from the windows, and later, grown older, her hair cropped,
the axe in her hands, swift, coming down on wood
from the careless pile, and him silent in shade, a rusted
chair, his used-up hands spotted with scars. In her mind
he would hear the axe's cough, the wind that slowed

with the sun's going, the train hauling its load through
the canyon, the pines throwing their thin silence down.
And in the kitchen she'd turn the calendar to another month,
shouting out the date for him as winter nagged the corners
of the house, and beyond the window, the horse with its tail
flying in black strands. Yes, she thought, she would stay until
the night like a blind pulled over his face,

until like a broken road he lay down, and she
alone again in the world. A bony girl staring out across a field.
And she would know, finally, what love was. And take
a lover then, lie naked on top of the sheets, her hand
on his chest, and tell him of the old man, how she stayed
and stayed. But she'd change the story just enough,
not wanting to give him that beauty. Not yet.

Saying instead, *I was a seed, a tattered thing*
*fallen from the sky, a feather with wings.*
*Now I grow underground, a root, a ruin, a house,*
*grave and solemn as stone.*

IV.

Her loneliness said *return*, but by then the dam covered
the canyon with its dark cloth. Standing on the precipice,
she remembered everything: how once, she was a girl
who lay on her back in a barn, and the canyon filled with sky,
a sea whose fish were named sparrow, swallow, osprey, owl.
An old man opened his door and she walked in.

How the windows broke the sky into pieces. How daisies'
hard spines cracked the dirt, their faces peered over the sill.
The kitchen clock's two stiffened fingers. The tractor
whose colour the wind stole, its wheels filled with mice
and straw. Sparrow's tracks in snow. The pile of field stones.
And he, bitten thin by weather.

And she thought of the two hearts, horse and man,

buried under the new sea. The fractured steps
he stumbled down at the end. The moon, too, drowned.
Only its light rising from the water.
And if the old man was hungry or thirsty, he could tell no one
but the thousand mouths of stone. He, the night watchman
of his own small room, his pine box bed.

Each noon and night he'd left the fist of his napkin
on the plate. She listened for the hay fork waiting by the barn,
for the small silent boats, birds, but could hear no song.
And wondered if fallen apples could rise like a question.

In the days that passed she dreamt herself underwater, curtains
billowing over her bed, the willow waving in the yard.
Back then, she thought they were poor. Then she remembered
how lilac bloomed among barbed wire.
Once, she was a girl.

# Here, the watersheds are called

**Wendy Morton**

DeMamiel
Veitch
Charters
Wildwood.
The creeks:
Sombrio
Loss
Sandcut
Kirby
Muir
Tugwell
King
Juliet.

Then: cut blocks, clearcuts; grapple skidder, feller buncher, crawler dozer.
The liquidated landscape, broken,
the creeks, lost.
The watersheds, their forests, a wasteland.

# WITH NO SWEET WATER
## 水调歌头·难溯甘泉

**Cynthia Woodman Kerkham**

*in response to Li Xinmo's photographic series "The Death of Xinkai River"*
*with translation by Liu Xia/Tang Haiyue*

1.

What would the ancient poets say of poisoned Xinkai river?
Wang Wei and Li Bai exiled on state business,

> wine-drunk and swapping lines beside a green stream.
> 毒淖几曾有? 太白问摩诘。

We know poison, they might say, as when Empress Wei
fouled her husband's veins to put her son on the throne.

> We know fire ships, blazing rivers in the time of Warring States.
> 却道韦氏帝梦, 战火连营间。

But burning rivers marked a time of war, though perhaps,
it is always a time of war. We know the Emperors of greed,

> their creeping slaughter of the river-huddled peasant.
> 太平盛世如梦, 又添百姓疾苦, 何处无民怨。

Pass the jug, they might shout,

> with no sweet water, exile.
> 辗转过山岳, 此世无甘泉。

2.

Black-haired girl in a white shift,
belly down, face partially submerged.

> How to love a stinging stream? Photograph yourself in it.
> 素衣白, 青丝黛, 沉朱颜。

Blue-green algae petals her bare shoulders.
Dead-woman river; dark-hair weeds,

> close-up skin lined in burning rills.
> 青荇缠绕, 玉陨冰肌江水燃。

How to recover from phosphorous, nitrogen?
River as waste. Septic
        waterway unfurls to the sea.

Xin, meaning New. Kai, Open.
Newly Opened River now closed.
        Condos and factories its riparian zone.
        浊水又见新居。

Blue-green algae born from the dark,
viridian pearls lacing the dead woman's hand. Witness
        in the click of a shutter.
        快门闪过人言, 树影惊魍怜。

3.
The river is weary. A muddy green
thickens its once-shimmering blood.
        The willow no longer strokes its cheek.

The men fishing from the mound
fertile with apricot trees are ghostly shadows.
        Imperial officials hold high meetings

while Xinkai hurts for the white-nosed sturgeon.
Ah, its cool-moon body,
        the rustle and tickle of fin.
        新开河上冷, 华堂声正喧。

# Desert Fish

**Joanna Lilley**

*for the Tecopa Pupfish*

Water warms
as it mingles, as it gushes,
heats
the cyan pupfish eating
hot blue-green algae,
teething mosquito larvae.

The Amargosa River hot springs,
—enlarged, diverted, merged—
submerge the salt rush, needlerush,

unplanting pickleweed,
parching pluvial pools

until wedges of striped, olive-brown fish
float,
swelling to rot,

dying for another species' bathhouse wallow,
with parking on Noonday Street,

pubic hair coiled in foot-churned mud,
hot bare shoulders powdered in sunset,

as the moon rolls across Death Valley,
smack into the decay of Vegas.

# HER VOICE A FORGE

**Marlene Grand Maître**

A bald porcelain doll's head cradled
in her left palm, a woman strides,

jaywalks during rush hour on Douglas Street.
She could be our Cassandra, Earth the small orb

cupped in her hand. Her voice a forge,
tempers unheeded watershed warnings.

        She keens in the dialect
of parched streams and rivers—
Koksilah, Chemainus, San Juan, Salmon.

        Keens in the dialect of *river piracy*—
the Kaskawulsh glacier melts, the Slims River
vanishes, its direction changed overnight.

But the flow of traffic stops for no prophet.
Drivers honk, give her the finger.

        Insulated by steel and glass
on a double-decker bus, we drift above
our bodies, slumped on seats,

        orphans waiting to be claimed,
skulls vulnerable as a newborn's fontanelle

# CATCHING RAIN IN A PAPER BAG

**Rhonda Ganz**

Because I loved water, father loved me best. Body of water.
Body of evidence. My father face-down at water's edge.

Foul play is not suspected. If missing is the same as disappeared,
I disappear my father's face, his waders, frogsong and the putt-putt

of his Evinrude short-shaft as we crossed the lake home.
Cross out lake, cross out stream, cross out marsh

at lake's edge where the cattails grow. Carve the word *tadpole*
into the rock wall at the far end of the lake. The future needs a name

for shallow imprints of back legs and a tail in layers of
hardened sediment. Under sidewalk, under cul-de-sac,

under parking lot, a fossil trail from used-to-be-lake
down used-to-be-stream. My father showed me where water went

to die. We would lie down in the middle of the road,
ears pressed to the pavement, "Here," he'd say,

"There used to be a pond here. A heron once stood still here."
Red-winged blackbirds and cattails and jesus bugs out of the lexicon.

In the official version, my father drowns. In mine, he gives his last breath
to the lake trout, imploring them to grow eyelids and elbows.

Adapt or die. Lake trout and my father out of the lexicon.
This happened in a past life. Drownings now as rare as leprosy.

A bathtub on display in the water museum labelled artifact: 21st century.
In this life, I am having trouble swallowing liquids.

Have as many children as you can, my doctor says,
you are evolving to eat sand.

# WALK TO THE WETLANDS

**Diana Hayes**

All summer the drought begged me to stay put
not wander the matchstick dryness for fear of disturbing
invisible cairns, the long walk to the wetlands.

Desiccated flora, cattails becoming straw
deflecting a hint of breeze while
dry mouths gather at the edge
of a lake once bottomless.

Each evening the geese join families,
pass overhead with familiar ease and wing beat.
Winter's old stream bed a semaphore of rock
spreading like a fan toward the wetlands.

Is that the ghost of rushing water,
memory flowing past the southern knoll?
A wraith of rain bathing a chorus of frogs?

Open me like a book, I say to the poet
praising the tiny nameless flowers
insects and acorns that fill the forest night.

I am all ears, I say to the poet.
If I speak your words, over and over again
will your wisdom bring rain,
your praise light up a new morning?

lake visit
after 30 years
my memory of the loon

**kjmunro**,
Canim Lake, Cariboo

# Bios

**Maleea Acker** is the author of two poetry collections, *The Reflecting Pool* and *Air-Proof Green* (Pedlar, 2009, 2013), and the non-fiction book *Gardens Aflame: Garry Oak Meadows of BC's South Coast* (New Star Books, 2012). She teaches Geography and Canadian Studies at the University of Victoria, where she is a PhD candidate in Geopoetics.

**Solveig Adair** is a college instructor and writer who loves the North in all its forms and complexities. She has been published in several literary journals and anthologies including *filling Station* and *Beyond Forgetting: Celebrating 100 Years of Al Purdy* from Harbour Publishing. Wherever she has lived and travelled, the waters of the North have always called her home.

**Susan Alexander** lives and writes in the Howe Sound/Atl'kitsem watershed on the traditional territory of the Squamish Nation. Much of her work is rooted in a keen, even holy, sense of place, yet place is often haunted by anxiety over a precarious present, an uncertain future and how the self is implicated in these complexities. Susan's poems have appeared in chapbooks and several literary magazines. She is the author of *The Dance Floor Tilts* (Thistledown Press, 2017). Her poems have received three awards and one poem is currently riding the Vancouver buses (Poetry in Transit, 2018-19).

**Laurel Apol** is an associate professor at Michigan State University. Her poetry appears in numerous anthologies and literary journals, and she is recognized through a number of poetry prizes. She is the author of four full-length collections, most recently *Nothing but the Blood* (Michigan State University Press, 2018; winner of the Oklahoma Book Award for poetry), and she was recently selected to serve as the Lansing-area poet laureate.

**John Barton**'s twenty-six books, chapbooks, monographs, and anthologies include *Seminal: The Anthology of Canada's Gay-Male Poets, For the Boy with the Eyes of the Virgin: Selected Poems, Polari, The Malahat Review at Fifty, The Essential Douglas LePan,* and *We Are Not Avatars: Essays, Memoirs, Manifestos.* In 2020, he will publish *The Essential Derk Wynand,* and a book of sonnets, *Lost Family.* Born in Edmonton and raised in Calgary, he lives in Victoria, where he is the city's fifth, first male, and first queer poet laureate.

Hamilton writer, musician and multimedia artist **Gary Barwin** is the author of twenty-two books including the nationally bestselling novel *Yiddish for Pirates*, winner of the Leacock Medal for Humour, the Canadian Jewish Literary Award, and finalist for the Scotiabank Giller Prize and the Governor General's Award. His poetry includes *For It is a Pleasure and a Surprise to Breathe: New and Selected Poems*, ed. Alessandro Porco (Wolsak & Wynn, 2019) and, with Tom Prime, *A Cemetery for Holes* (Gordon Hill, 2019) A new novel, *Nothing the Same, Everything Haunted* will appear Spring 2021. garybarwin.com.

**Lee Beavington** is a poet-scientist-philosopher. He is an award-winning author, educator and PhD candidate in Philosophy of Education at SFU with a focus on environmental ethics. He has taught a wide range of courses and labs at Kwantlen Polytechnic University, including the Amazon Field School. Find Lee reflecting in the forest, mesmerized by ferns, and always following the river. More about Lee at www.leebeavington.com.

Victoria writer **Barbara Black** was recently nominated by Don't Talk To Me About Love for the 2019 Journey Prize. Her work won first prize in both the 2018 Federation of BC Writers Literary Writes and 2017 Writers' Union of Canada Short Prose competitions. Also a recipient of first prize in the 2017 Don't Talk To Me About Love Poetry Contest, her poems have appeared in *Contemporary Verse 2* and the League of Canadian Poets anthology *Heartwood*. www.barbarablack.ca, @barbarablackwriter, and #bblackwrites.

**Robert Boates** was born in Hamilton, Ontario and grew up there. He wrote his first poem in grade 8. In 1989 when he was living in Hamilton again, he suffered a serious brain injury after a fall down an illegal set of stairs. After he awoke from a coma, Robert had little physical functionality, but he could write poetry. Continuing to recover, Robert provides a literary voice for survivors of head injury, documenting his passage in a second life. His poetry has been published in Japan, England, the United States and Canada. His books include *The Good life* (Cactus Tree Press), *The Afterlife* (Seraphim Editions) and *He Carries Fear* (Cactus Tree Press).

**Nicholas Bradley** is a poet, literary critic, and scholarly editor. His most recent book is *Rain Shadow*, a collection of poems published by the University of Alberta Press. He lives in Victoria, British Columbia.

**Kate Braid** has written, co-written, edited and co-edited fourteen books and chapbooks of creative non-fiction and prize-winning poetry, most recently *Elemental* (Caitlin Press, 2018). She also co-edited with Sandy Shreve the ground-breaking anthology of Canadian form poetry, *In Fine Form*.

**Terri Brandmueller** is a former newspaper journalist and food writer, currently working on a creative non-fiction book about family secrets and Internet genealogy. Her poetry and fiction have appeared in various publications in the US, Canada, and the UK. She studied journalism at Langara, literature and cultural studies at the New School for Social Research in NYC, and has an MA in Media Studies. She lives in East Vancouver where she holds a monthly reading salon.

**Brian Brett**, former chair of the Writers' Union of Canada and a journalist for decades, is best known as a poet, memoir writer, and fictionist. His thirteen books include his memoir, *Uproar's Your Only Music*, a *Globe and Mail* Book of The Year selection. *Trauma Farm: A Rebel History of Rural Life*, won numerous prizes, including the Writers' Trust annual award for non-fiction. A collection of poems, *The Wind River Variations* was released in 2014. And the final book in his trilogy of memoirs, *Tuco*, was published in 2015 and was awarded the Hubert Evans Non-Fiction Prize.

**Michelle Poirier Brown** is a Cree Métis poet and photographer from Manitoba, currently living in Lekwungen territory. Her poem "Wake" was published in the *PRISM international* "Dreams" issue, and awarded the Earle Birney Prize. Other work has appeared in *CV2*, *Grain,* and *Dis(s)ent: An Anthology Curating Difficult Knowledge* (In/Words Magazine & Press). Long list awards for poetry include Grouse Grind Lit Prize for V(ery) Short Forms, Literary Writes, and *This Magazine*'s National Poetry Competition. Her short fiction has been long listed for Canadian Authors Association and *PRISM international* competitions.

**Jenna Butler** is the author of the award-winning poetry books *Seldom Seen Road, Wells,* and *Aphelion*; the essay collection *A Profession of Hope: Farming on the Edge of the Grizzly Trail*; and a new poetic travelogue, *Magnetic North: Sea Voyage to Svalbard*. Her research into endangered environments has taken her from America's Deep South to Ireland's Ring of Kerry, and from volcanic Tenerife to the Arctic Circle, documenting human impact on lands under threat. A professor at Red Deer College, Butler lives with seven resident moose and a den of coyotes on an off-grid organic farm in northern Alberta.

**Claire Caldwell** lives in Toronto, where she writes, edits children's books at Annick Press, and runs poetry workshops for kids. Her second poetry collection, about women in the wilderness, is forthcoming from Invisible Publishing in Spring 2020. Her first book, *Invasive Species*, was published by Wolsak & Wynn in 2014. Claire was a 2016 writer in residence at the Berton House in Dawson City, Yukon, and the 2013 winner of The Malahat Review's Long Poem Prize. She has an MFA from the University of Guelph.

**Trevor Carolan**'s books include poetry, non-fiction, novels, and journalism. He has produced documentary films and works frequently with musicians. His co-edited Eco-lit edition *Cascadia: The Life and Breath of the World,* received a Best American Essays 2013 Citation. A former elected Councillor in North Vancouver, he fought successfully to preserve the North Shore's Cove and Mountain forests as wilderness, and was instrumental in shepherding the Lower Seymour Conservation Area and the Varley Trail at Lynn Canyon Headwaters into being. He has worked on behalf of Indigenous land claims and teaches at UFV near Vancouver. More at: www.trevorcarolan.com.

Poet and paper artist **Terry Ann Carter** has published seven collections of poetry and five chapbooks of haiku. She is the past president of Haiku Canada and facilitator for the Haiku Arbutus Study Group of Victoria.

**Karen Charleson** is a mother, a grandmother, a writer, and an educator. Her first novel, *Through Different Eyes,* was published by Signature Editions in 2017. Karen is a member, through marriage, of the Hesquiaht First Nation and the House of Kinquashtakumtlth. She lives in Hesquiat Harbour on the west coast of Vancouver Island with her husband, Stephen Charleson.

**Karen Chester** lives and writes in Victoria, B.C. The Westcoast—its waters, forests, creatures, characters, and contradictions—finds all kinds of ways to sneak into poems. Karen's poetry has aired on CBC Radio, and has been published in *Rocksalt: An Anthology of Contemporary BC Poetry*; in *Poems from Planet Earth*; and in two chapbooks edited by Patrick Lane (*Radiant Among Yellow Willows* and *What's Left Between Us*).

**Daniel Cowper** is the author *Grotesque Tenderness,* a book of poetry published in 2019 by MQUP. A chapbook of his poetry, *The God of Doors,* was published in 2017 as winner of Frog Hollow Press' chapbook contest. His poetry has been published in *Arc, Vallum, Prairie Fire*, and other literary publications, and in 2017 he was long-listed for the CBC poetry Prize. He lives on Bowen Island, BC, with his wife, Emily Osborne, and their son.

**xavier o. datura** is just another peasant—he can swing a pen like a blade tho.

**Lauren Elle DeGaine** (she/her) obtained her BA in Writing and Literature from Naropa University's Jack Kerouac School in Colorado. Lauren attended the Emerging Writers Intensive at the Banff Centre for Arts and Creativity in 2017. Her chapbook, *The Landscape We Left on Each Other,* was published by The Blasted Tree in 2018. Her poetry, essays, interviews, and articles have appeared in or are forthcoming from *filling Station, Inverted Syntax*, and *NŌD Magazine*.

**Wendy Donawa** grew up in Victoria, but spent most of her adult life in Barbados, where she was an educator and museum curator. Since her return to BC, her poems have appeared in Canadian literary magazines, anthologies, and chapbooks. She is a contributing editor for *Arc Poetry Magazine* and a supporter of Planet Earth Poetry, Victoria's Friday night poetry reading series. Her début collection, *Thin Air of the Knowable* was longlisted for the 2018 Raymond Souster and shortlisted for the 2018 Gerald Lampert awards.

**Daniela Elza** was born on one continent, grew up on another, and now lives on a third. Her poetry collections are *the weight of dew, the book of It*, and *milk tooth bane bone*, of which David Abram says: "Out of the ache of the present moment, Daniela Elza has crafted something spare and irresistible, an open armature for wonder." Her essay "Bringing the Roots Home" was nominated for the 2018 Pushcart Prize. Her next poetry collection, *the broken boat,* is forthcoming in the spring of 2020. Daniela works as a Writer-in-Residence at the Bolton Academy for Spoken Arts.

**Dorothy Field** is a visual artist as well as the author of three books of poetry, the most recent *The Blackbird Must Be.* For the last several years she has been part of a group working to daylight a creek that rises in Victoria's Fernwood neighbourhood and flows into the Gorge.

**Heather Fraser** is a poet and public service worker living on the traditional lands of the Lekwungen Nation. She holds a Bachelor of Fine Arts in writing from the University of Victoria. Her poetry has previously appeared in *This Side of West, Poetry Lives Here, Poetry is Dead, Grain Magazine*, and *Prairie Fire*.

**Art Fredeen** is a plant ecophysiologist and professor in the Ecosystem Science and Management program at the University of Northern British Columbia in Prince George. He has been writing haiku for nearly twenty-two years, most of them inspired by nature, allowing him to explore and express the beauty of the things he studies.

**Rhonda Ganz**'s first book of poetry, *Frequent, Small Loads of Laundry* (Mother Tongue, 2017) was a finalist for the 2018 Dorothy Livesay Poetry Prize and the Victoria Butler Book Prize. Her poems have appeared in *The Malahat Review, Rattle,* and *Harvard Design Magazine,* on buses, and in the anthologies *Rocksalt, Poems from Planet Earth, Poet to Poet, Erotic Haiku: Of Skin on Skin* and *Force Field: 77 Women Poets of BC.* She has been a featured reader at numerous events and festivals.

**Kim Goldberg** is the author of eight books of poetry and nonfiction. Her poems have appeared in *Literary Review of Canada, The Capilano Review, Prairie Fire, sub-Terrain* and elsewhere. Her latest collection is *Devolution* (Caitlin Press, 2020), poems of the ecopocalypse. Kim holds a degree in biology, and she chaired the women's ecopoetry panel at the inaugural Cascadia Poetry Festival in Seattle. She lives in Nanaimo, BC, near a small river where salmon still spawn. Twitter: @KimPigSquash

**Alisa Gordaneer** writes poetry, teaches at Vancouver Island University and Royal Roads University, and works as a communications consultant. Her first full-length collection of poems, *Still Hungry,* was published in 2015.

**Ariel Gordon** is the author of two collections of urban-nature poetry, both of which won the Lansdowne Prize for Poetry at the Manitoba Book Awards. Recent projects include the anthology *GUSH: menstrual manifestos for our times,* co-edited with Tanis MacDonald and Rosanna Deerchild, and the fifth installment of the National Poetry Month in the *Winnipeg Free Press* project. Her most recent books are *Treed: Walking in Canada's Urban Forests* (Wolsak & Wynn, 2019) and *TreeTalk: Winnipeg* (At Bay Press, 2020). She lives in Winnipeg, Manitoba.

**Laurie D. Graham** is a writer, editor, and the publisher of *Brick* magazine. She is the author of *Rove* and *Settler Education,* as well as the chapbook *The Larger Forgetting,* a collaborative project with painter Amanda Rhodenizer. Laurie hails from Treaty 6 territory (Sherwood Park, Alberta) and now lives in Treaty 20 territory (Peterborough, Ontario), a very watery place.

**Marlene Grand Maître**'s poetry has been published in literary journals such as *The Malahat Review, Grain, The Antigonish Review, Event,* and *CV2.* A poem was longlisted for *Best Canadian Poetry In English 2011* (Tightrope Books), and her work has also appeared in five anthologies, most recently in *Refugium: Poems for the Pacific* (Caitlin Press, 2017). Her poetry is forthcoming in *Voicing Suicide* (Ekstasis Editions, 2020). She has won prizes, including Freefall's 2013 poetry competition, and the Federation of BC Writers' 2015 poetry prize. A grateful guest on the unceded traditional territory of the Lkwungen people, she lives in Esquimalt, BC.

**Raine Gutierrez** has travelled across the world, from North America to Asia, and has lived in a total of four cities. When she was younger, she was obsessed with dinosaurs and wanted to become an author. Raine now resides in Victoria where she attends high school with many of her best friends. She loves to write poetry often inspired by the beautiful Vancouver Island landscape and go running along Victoria's breathtaking shorelines. She thanks Jamie Burren and Anita Roberts for helping her grow as a writer and Megan Thom for telling her about this amazing writing opportunity.

**gillian harding-russell** is a Regina poet, freelance writer, reviewer and editor. She has five chapbooks and four poetry collections published, most recently *In Another Air* (Radiant Press, 2018), which was shortlisted for a Saskatchewan Book Award. In 2016, "Making Sense" was chosen as best suite in *Exile*'s Gwendolyn MacEwen chapbook award. Poems have recently appeared in *Heartwood* ed. Lesley Strutt (LCP publication, 2018), and will soon appear in *Resistance,* ed. Sue Goyette (Coteau Books)

Poet and essayist **Maureen Scott Harris** was born in Prince Rupert, BC, grew up in Winnipeg and has lived in Toronto since the 1960s. She's been a freelance writer and editor, librarian, bookstore clerk, and production manager for Brick Books Her publications include three collections of poetry and three chapbooks, as well as work in Canadian, American, British, and Australian journals. Her essay on the Don River won the WildCare Tasmania Nature Writing Prize. With the River Poets she has developed poetry walks through Toronto's ravines and parks.

**Richard Harrison** is the author of seven books of poetry, among them the Governor General's Award-winning *On Not Losing My Father's Ashes in the Flood* (Wolsak & Wynn, 2016). His work has been translated into five languages, including a complete Italian translation of that book. He has contributed essays and poetry to the writing on comics and graphic novels, hockey, and ecopoetics. He teaches English and Creative Writing at Calgary's Mount Royal University.

**Diana Hayes** was born in Toronto and has lived on both coasts of Canada. She studied at UBC and UVic, receiving a BA and MFA in Creative Writing. Her fifth collection of poems, *Labyrinth of Green*, was published by Plumleaf Press, Summer 2019. Her poetry was included in the anthologies *Rocksalt, Force Field* and *111 West Coast Literary Portraits*. Her narrative photography has been commissioned for book covers and featured in galleries in coastal BC. Her practice of year-round ocean swimming inspired the formation of the Salt Spring Seals in 2002. Salt Spring Island has been home since 1981. www.dianahayes.ca

**Steven Heighton**'s most recent poetry collection, *The Waking Comes Late*, received the 2016 Governor General's Award for Poetry. His short fiction and poetry have received four gold National Magazine Awards and have appeared in *London Review of Books, Best English Stories, Poetry, Best American Poetry, Tin House, TLR, Agni, Best American Mystery Stories, Zoetrope, London Magazine, New England Review*, and many editions of *Best Canadian Stories* and *Best Canadian Poetry*. Heighton is also an occasional fiction reviewer for the *New York Times* Book Review.

**Iain Higgins** lives a short walk away from a buried creek in Saanich, British Columbia, where the Songhees, Esquimalt, and W̱SÁNEĆ peoples have cared for the unceded lands and waters since time immemorial.

**Bruce Hunter** is the author of seven books, including the novel *In the Bear's House* (Oolichan Books, 2009), winner of the Canadian Rockies Prize at the Banff Mountain Film and Book Festival, chosen from over one hundred entries from ten countries, and *Two O'clock Creek: Poems New and Selected* (Oolichan Books, 2010), winner of the Acorn/Plantos Peoples' Poetry Prize. His poem "Two O'clock Creek" was the "seed" poem that inspired his novel set in the headwaters of the Upper North Saskatchewan River on the eastern slopes of the Canadian Rockies. In 2017, Bruce was the Calgary Public Library's 30th anniversary Author in Residence.

**Maureen Hynes**'s first book of poetry, *Rough Skin*, won the League of Canadian Poets' Gerald Lampert Award for best first book of poetry by a Canadian. Her 2016 collection, *The Poison Colour*, was shortlisted for both the Pat Lowther and Raymond Souster Awards. Maureen's fifth book of poetry, *Sotto Voce*, came out from Brick Books in Autumn, 2019. Her poetry has been included in over twenty-five anthologies, including twice in *Best Canadian Poems in English*, and in *Best of the Best Canadian Poetry, 2017*. Maureen is poetry editor for *Our Times* magazine.

**Ishtar** lives with illnesses, physical and mental, and the effects of trauma including from residential school for the blind, sexual violence, abuse, exclusion, other. They experience isolation because of illness, ableism, poverty and inadequate health-care. They are an activist focussing on equality, clarity, authenticity and interrupting ableism. Ishtar cares deeply about our relationships with and treatment of people, decolonization, and actual reconciliation, and our relationships with other species and ecosystems. Ishtar urges you to speak, ask difficult questions, listen, pay attention then carefully act for the long-term planetary benefit, even when it is not convenient; practise tenderness with accountability.

**M.W. Jaeggle** is the author of two chapbooks, *Janus on the Pacific* (Baseline Press, 2019) and *The Night of the Crash* (Alfred Gustav Press, 2019). His writing has appeared in *The Antigonish Review*, *CV2*, *The Dalhousie Review*, *Vallum*, and elsewhere. Educated at Simon Fraser University and McGill University, he lives in Vancouver, unceded Coast Salish territory.

**Elena Johnson** is the author of *Field Notes for the Alpine Tundra* (Gaspereau, 2015), a collection of poems written at a remote ecology research station in the Yukon. A finalist for the CBC Literary Awards and the Alfred G. Bailey Prize, her work has been published in many journals and anthologies, including *The Fiddlehead*, *ARC*, *Lemon Hound* and *Best Canadian Poetry in English*. Her poems have also been set to music and performed by the Vancouver Chamber Choir and the Brooklyn Youth Choir. Originally from New Brunswick, she now lives in Vancouver.

**Alyse Knorr** is an assistant professor of English at Regis University and, since 2017, co-editor of Switchback Books. Her most recent book of poems, *Mega-City Redux*, won the 2016 Green Mountains Review Poetry Prize, selected by Olena Kalytiak Davis. She is also the author of the poetry collections *Copper Mother* (Switchback Books, 2016) and *Annotated Glass* (Furniture Press Books, 2013); the non-fiction book *Super Mario Bros. 3* (Boss Fight Books, 2016); and the poetry chapbooks *Epithalamia* (Horse Less Press, 2015) and *Alternates* (dancing girl press, 2014). Her work has appeared in *Alaska Quarterly Review*, *Denver Quarterly*, *The Greensboro Review*, and *ZYZZYVA*, among others.

For almost thirty years, **Beth Kope** has lived and worked in Victoria, a grateful visitor to the traditional territories of the Coast Salish Nation. She has raised a family, walked dogs and written poems as a call-response to the landscape around her. She is the author of two books (*Falling Season*, *Average Height of Flight*) with another book on the way. Wherever she's been, she's found a lake to swim in.

**Elee Kraljii Gardiner** is the author of the poetry collections *Trauma Head* (Anvil Press, 2018), a chapbook of the same name (Otter Press, 2017), *serpentine loop* (Anvil Press, 2016), and the anthologies *Against Death: 35 Essays on Living* (Anvil Press, 2019) and *V6A: Writing from Vancouver's Downtown Eastside* (Arsenal Pulp Press, 2012). She founded Thursdays Writing Collective, a beloved non-profit organization, and through its ten years she edited and published nine of its anthologies. She is an MFA candidate in poetry at the Institute for American Indian Arts. eleekg.com

**Aaron Kreuter** is the author of the 2018 short story collection *You and Me, Belonging,* and the poetry collection *Arguments for Lawn Chairs.* He lives in Toronto, where he is working on a novel set at a Jewish sleepover camp.

**Anita Lahey**'s books include *The Mystery Shopping Cart: Essays on Poetry and Culture* (Palimpsest Press, 2013) and two Véhicule Press poetry collections: *Spinning Side Kick* and *Out to Dry in Cape Breton.* Anita is also a journalist and series editor of the *Best Canadian Poetry in English* anthology. Her memoir, *The Last Goldfish: A true tale of friendship,* is forthcoming from Biblioasis. She lives in Ottawa.

**Fiona Tinwei Lam**'s third book of poetry, *Odes & Laments* (Caitlin Press, 2019), includes several poems about human incursions on the natural world. She edited *The Bright Well: Canadian Poems on Facing Cancer,* and co-edited *Love Me True: Writers on the Ins, Outs, Ups & Downs of Marriage.* Her work appears in over thirty anthologies, including *The Best Canadian Poetry in English* and *Forcefield: 77 Women Poets of BC.* Her poetry videos have screened at festivals locally and internationally. She teaches at Simon Fraser University's Continuing Studies. fionalam.net

**Zoë Landale** has published eight books, edited two books, and her work appears in somewhere around fifty anthologies. Her writing has won significant awards in three genres, including first in the Stony Brook University Short Fiction competition, National Magazine Gold for memoir, and first in the CBC Literary Competition for poetry. She taught for fifteen years as a faculty member in the Creative Writing Department at Kwantlen Polytechnic University in Vancouver, British Columbia. Landale's latest book of poetry, *Sigrene's Bargain with Odin,* is forthcoming with Inanna Press.

**Joanna Lilley** is the author of three poetry collections: *Endlings* (Turnstone Press, 2020), *If There Were Roads* (Turnstone Press, 2017) and *The Fleece Era* (Brick Books, 2014) which was nominated for the Fred Cogswell Award for Excellence in Poetry.

She's also the author of a novel, *Worry Stones* (Ronsdale Press, 2018), which was longlisted for the Caledonia Novel Award, and a short story collection, *The Birthday Books* (Hagios Press, 2015). Joanna is from the UK and now lives in Whitehorse, Yukon, where she's grateful to reside on the Traditional Territories of the Kwanlin Dün First Nation and the Ta'an Kwäch'än Council.

**D.A. Lockhart** is the author of five collections of poetry, including most recently *Devil in the Woods* (Brick Books, 2019) and *The Gravel Lot that was Montana* (Mansfield Press, 2018). His work has received generous financial support from the Ontario Arts Council and the Canada Council for the Arts. Lockhart holds a MFA in Creative Writing from Indiana University Bloomington. He is a turtle clan citizen of the Moravian of Thames First Nation. He currently splits his time between Pelee Island and Waawiiyaataanong where he is the publisher at Urban Farmhouse Press.

**Christine Lowther** is the author of *Born Out of This* (Caitlin Press, 2014), a memoir that was shortlisted for a BC Book Prize. Her poetry books are *Half-Blood Poems*, *My Nature*, and *New Power*. She is co-editor of *Writing the West Coast: In Love with Place* and *Living Artfully: Reflections from the Far West Coast*. Her work has appeared in *Rising Tides*, *The Summer Book*, *Canadian Ginger*, *Force Field: 77 Women Poets of British Columbia*, *Canada's Raincoast at Risk*, *The Malahat Review* and *Room* among others. Chris was grateful to receive the inaugural Rainy Coast Arts Award for Significant Accomplishment.

**Tanis MacDonald** is the author of five books of poetry and essays, including *Mobile* (Book*hug, 2019) and *Out of Line: Daring to Be an Artist Outside the Big City* (Wolsak & Wynn, 2018). She is co-editor, with Rosanna Deerchild and Ariel Gordon, of the anthology *GUSH: menstrual manifestos for our times* (Frontenac, House 2018).

**Dan MacIsaac** is the author of *Cries from the Ark*, published by Brick Books. His poetry has appeared in many journals, including *The Malahat Review, Arc, Vallum* and *CV2*. His website is danmacisaac.com.

**Adelia (Nicola) MacWilliam** recently completed her MFA in poetry at the University of Victoria. She wrote about a piece of land on Salt Spring Island that her family had "occupied" since 1905 and learned that if you cast the mythic imagination across a piece of land that has always been part of your life, everything will work out. She is co-founder of Cascadia Poetics Lab (www.cascadiapoeticslab.ca), which produces annual poetry events in Cumberland, and the monthly Red Tree reading series. She divides her time between Cumberland and Desolation Sound.

**Murray Mann** grew up in Fraser Lake BC. He has one poem published with *Island Writer*. Murray lives in Cobble Hill, BC, with his four kids.

**David Martin** works as a literacy instructor in Calgary and as an organizer for the Single Onion Poetry Series. His first poetry collection, *Tar Swan* (NeWest Press, 2018), was a finalist for the W. O. Mitchell Book Prize and the Raymond Souster Award. His work has been awarded the CBC Poetry Prize and his poems appeared in *The Malahat Review, Canadian Literature, The Fiddlehead, Grain, EVENT, CV2, filling Station,* and *Alberta Views.*

**Ilona Martonfi** is a Montreal poet born in Budapest. She is the author of five poetry books, *Blue Poppy* (Coracle, 2009), *Black Grass* (Broken Rules, 2012), *The Snow Kimono* (Inanna, 2015), *Salt Bride* (Inanna, 2019) and *The Tempest* (Inanna, 2020). She was a nominee for the 2018 Pushcart Prize for the poem "Dachau Visit on a Rainy Day". Founder / Artistic Director of The Yellow Door and Visual Arts Centre Reading Series.

**Rhona McAdam** is a poet, holistic nutritionist and food writer with a thirst for sustainable living. She has a master's degree in Food Culture from the University of Gastronomic Sciences (Slow Food's university in northern Italy), is a longtime volunteer with Haliburton Community Organic Farm, teaches Eco-Nutrition and manages the Victoria branch of the Canadian School of Natural Nutrition. Her most recent fulllength poetry collection, *Ex-Ville,* was published in 2014, and Rocky Mountain Books published her urban agriculture manifesto, *Digging the City,* in 2012.

**Wendy McGrath**'s most recent novel, *Broke City* (NeWest Press, 2019), is the final book in her Santa Rosa Trilogy. Her most recent book of poetry, *A Revision of Forward,* was released in Fall 2015. BOX (CD) 2017 is an adaptation of her long poem into spoken word/experimental jazz/noise by QUARTO & SOUND. MOVEMENT 1 from that CD was nominated for a 2018 Edmonton Music Award (Jazz Recording of the Year). She recently completed a collaborative manuscript of poems inspired by the photography of Danny Miles, drummer for July Talk and Tongue Helmet. Her poetry, fiction, and non-fiction has been widely published.

**Lorin Medley** is a counsellor and writer from Comox, BC, published in *The Puritan, Portal, subTerrain* and *Refugium: Poems for the Pacific.* She won the 2014 Islands

Short Fiction Contest, the 2015 Books Matter poetry prize and was longlisted for the 2016 Prism International Poetry Contest.

**Wendy Morton** has been WestJet's Poet of the Skies, Chrysler's Poet of the Road. She has six books of poetry and a memoir. She created Random Acts of Poetry and has been awarded The Spirit Bear Award, The Colleen Thibaudeau Outstanding Contribution to poetry award. She is an Honorary Citizen of Victoria. She has been awarded the Meritorious Service Medal by the Governor General of Canada. She was awarded the Order of B.C. She is now the Poet Laureate for the Juan de Fuca. For nine years she has been working with First Nations students and their Elders, and has produced 21 books of the poems written by the students: www.theelder-project.com/home.html.

Originally from Vancouver, BC, **kjmunro** moved to the Yukon Territory in 1991. She is Membership Secretary for Haiku Canada & a member of the League of Canadian Poets. In 2014 she founded 'solstice haiku', a monthly haiku discussion group that she continues to facilitate. Since January 2018, she has created & curated a weekly blog feature for The Haiku Foundation's Troutswirl blog, now managed with guest editors. Her debut collection is *contractions* (Red Moon Press, 2019).

**Ulrike Narwani,** of Baltic-German heritage, grew up in Edmonton, and completed a PhD in Slavic Languages and Literatures in Toronto. She moved to Sidney, BC, after living abroad for many years. *Collecting Silence* (Ronsdale Press, 2017) is her debut volume of poetry. Ulrike's poetry has been published in *CV2*, *Vallum*, chapbooks edited by Patrick Lane, the anthology *Poems from Planet Earth*, and has won *Freefall's* contest. Haiku appear in anthologies such as *Erotic Haiku* and, most recently, in *Collected Haiku* (League of Canadian Poets' Haiku Poetry Contest, 2018). One of her poems travelled happily on BC Transit.

**Lorri Neilsen Glenn**'s award-winning book, *Following the River: Traces of Red River Women* (2017) gathers stories about her Ininiwak and Métis grandmothers and their contemporaries. Lorri is the author and contributing editor of fourteen titles of nonfiction and poetry, former Halifax Poet Laureate, Professor Emerita at Mount Saint Vincent University and a mentor in the University of King's College creative nonfiction MFA. Her workshops are offered across Canada. Lorri's poetry has been adapted for libretti; she's received awards for innovative teaching, research, her work in the arts, her poetry and essays. Lorri lives in Nova Scotia. @neilsenglenn @river2seashore.

**Thos Nesbitt** has lived, worked and written poetry in Nunavut, Quebec, Ontario and the Northwest Territories, but now resides in British Columbia (Vancouver). The poetry he writes comes from, and owes its existence to, all of these parts of Canada. "Childhood: Danford Lake" is part of a cycle of similarly-themed poems written over many years, entitled *Turn Round the Seasons*.

**Charlie Neyelle** is one of the Elders of the Sahtugot'ine. He lives in Déline, on the shores of Sahtu ("Great Bear Lake" in English), Northwest Territories. Charlie learned the story of the Water Heart from his Elders, when he was very young. From 2002 to 2005, Charlie acted as the intermediary between the other Elders of Déline and a "Great Bear Lake Working Group", which was preparing *The Water Heart: A Management plan for Great Bear Lake*. Thos Nesbitt, co-author of "The Water Heart," is a lawyer (retired), facilitator, planner and occasionally a poet, who worked with the Elders and the Working Group to develop a consensus on and draft the *Management Plan*, including the story of the Water Heart.

**Geoffrey Nilson** is the founder of poetry micropress, pagefiftyone. The author of four chapbooks, his poems and essays have appeared with *Coast Mountain Culture, CV2, The Capilano Review, Event, PRISM international, Lemon Hound, Glasgow Review of Books,* and others. Nilson holds a BA in Creative Writing from Kwantlen Polytechnic University, is an alumnus of the Banff Centre Wired Writing Studio, and has been shortlisted for *The Malahat Review* Far Horizons Award for Poetry and the Alfred G. Bailey Poetry Prize. He lives with his daughter in New Westminster on the unceded territory of the Qayqayt First Nation.

**Emily Olsen** is a graduate of the 2016 Simon Fraser University "Writers Studio" Program in Fiction. She continued with the Writers Studio in 2016-2017 as the Poetry genre's Mentor Apprentice. Emily has a poetry blog, is published in *emerge 16*–The Writer's Studio Anthology, in *Sustenance, Oratorealis,* and has been a feature contributor with Seaside Magazine. Emily is founder of *The Connection Project,* an annual mental health storytelling event. She leads creativity workshops and serves as a director at large for the Federation of BC Writers. Emily lives with her husband and children in W̱SÁNEĆ Territory on Vancouver Island, BC.

**Catherine Owen** has published fifteen collections of poetry and prose. Her blog is called Marrow Reviews; her home performance series, 94th Street Trobairitz. She was born in Vancouver, BC, and now lives in Edmonton, AB, with her four cats in a 1905 home called Delilah.

**Nancy Pagh** burst on to the literary scene as a teenager, publishing her first poem, "Is a Clam Clammy, or Is It Just Wet?" in a regional boating magazine. She earned a Master's in writing at the University of New Hampshire and a PhD at the University of British Columbia, where she wrote her thesis on accounts by women travelling the Northwest Coast by boat. She teaches at Western Washington University, recently publishing *Write Moves: A Creative Writing Guide & Anthology* based on her teaching experiences. Her poems appear in *Refugium, Canadian Literature, Rattle, Prairie Schooner,* and *Crab Creek Review.*

**Arleen Paré** is a Victoria writer. She has five collections of poetry, two of which are cross-genre. She has been short-listed for the Dorothy Livesay Poetry Prize, and has won a Golden Crown Award for Lesbian Poetry, a Victoria Butler Book Prize, a CBC Bookie Award, and a Governor General's Award for Poetry.

**John Pass**'s poems have appeared in Canada, the US, the UK, Ireland and the Czech Republic. He won the Governor General's Award in 2006 for *Stumbling in the Bloom* (Oolichan Books) and the Dorothy Livesay Poetry Prize (BC Book Award) for *crawlspace* (Harbour Publishing) in 2012. Recent titles, both from Harbour Publishing, are *Forecast* (Selected Early Poems 1970 – 1990) published in 2015, and a new collection, *This Was The River*, was released in Fall 2019. Pass lives on the Sunshine Coast with his wife, essayist and novelist, Theresa Kishkan.

**Jeremy Pataky** is the author of *Overwinter* (University of Alaska Press). His poetry and essays have appeared in journals including *Colorado Review, Black Warrior Review, The Southeast Review, Camas, Ice Floe, Anchorage Press,* and many others. Jeremy earned degrees at the University of Montana and Western Washington University. He is a founding former board member and Executive Director of 49 Writers, a literary nonprofit in the 49th state, and publisher of *Edible Alaska* magazine. He splits his time between McCarthy, Alaska, inside Wrangell-St. Elias National Park—part of a 24-million-acre World Heritage Site, the largest international protected area on the planet—and Anchorage.

**Barbara Pelman** is a retired English teacher living in Victoria. She was the winner of the Malahat Review Open Season Contest with her glosa, "Nevertheless", and winner of the BC Federation of Writers' poetry contest for the poem "Aubade Amalfi". She has three published books of poetry: *One Stone* (Ekstasis Editions, 2005); *Borrowed Rooms* (Ronsdale Press, 2008); and *Narrow Bridge* (Ronsdale Press, 2017); and a chapbook, *Aubade Amalfi* (Rubicon Press, 2016). Her poem "Blueberry Creek" is also a glosa, a form she loves for its strictures and its tribute to another poet.

**Kirsten Pendreigh** lives in the Capilano Watershed. Her poems appear in *Arc Poetry, Prairie Fire, subTerrain, CV2, Juniper Poetry, Room, Sea to Sky Review, Savant-Garde, Sustenance* Anthology (Anvil Press, 2017) and *Another Dysfunctional Cancer Poem* Anthology (Mansfield Press, 2018). She won the Pandora's Collective Poetry Contest in 2018 and is a two-time winner of the Whistler Poet's Pause competition. Her debut children's book *LET THE BABY PUSH THE BUTTONS!* will publish in 2021. On twitter: @kpiependreigh

Born in the UK, **David Pimm** is a quasi-retired individual living mostly in Vancouver, while shuttling weekly to Victoria to rehearse. Beside choral singing, writing poetry is his other major un-work action: for more than a decade, he has attended poetry retreats (in BC, Ontario and Newfoundland). David has had occasional poems published in literary journals such as *The Malahat Review* and *The Fiddlehead*, and in anthologies such as *Poems from Planet Earth, Refugium* and this one. Sometimes, these two non-employment passions of music and poetry overlap, not least with a growing number of poems attached to Bach's Cello Suites.

**Pamela Porter** is the author of fourteen published books—ten volumes of poetry and four books for children and young adults, including two novels in verse. Her work has earned more than a dozen provincial, national, and international awards, including the Governor General's Award for *The Crazy Man*, and appeared on CBC, Raymond Souster and Pat Lowther Award shortlists. Both *The Crazy Man* and her 2011 novel, *I'll Be Watching*, are required reading in schools and colleges across Canada and the US. Pamela lives near Sidney, BC, with her family and a menagerie of rescued horses, dogs, and cats.

**Marion Quednau** published *Paradise, Later Years*, a debut collection of poems with Caitlin Press in 2018. Her poetry appears in Poetry-in-Transit and in the *Best Canadian Poetry 2019* anthology (Biblioasis). Her work has previously won awards from the League of Canadian Poets for the chapbook, *Kissing: Selected Chronicles*, and the Long Poem Prize, Malahat Review, a National Magazine Award, Gold, and was short-listed for the CBC Poetry Prize in 2012, winning the People's Choice distinction. She lives on BC's Sunshine Coast, watching the "sweet water" run towards the sea.

**Brent Raycroft**'s poetry has appeared in *Prairie Fire, Arc, CV2, Vallum, Queen's Quarterly, The Broken City*, and elsewhere, including *The Best of the Best Canadian Poetry: Tenth Anniversary Edition*. A single-poem chapbook, *The Subtleties of Divine Creatures* was published by Thee Hellbox Press in 2014. In 2016 he self-published his short epic, *Sydenham*, to celebrate Canada 175. He lives north of Kingston, Ontario.

**D.C. Reid** is a past president of the League of Canadian Poets and Federation of BC Writers. His most recent awards are the National Roderick Haig-Brown award for sustained environmental writing and best poem in the *Love and War Anthology*. D.C. is also a fly fisherman with his fifth fishing book *A Man and His River*, stories of twenty-five years spent on the Nitinat River, Vancouver Island. He is at work on his eleventh book of poems, *Canada, A Country of Poets*, and an anthology of poets and poems, *Hologram for PK Page*, with Yvonne Blomer.

**Al Rempel**'s books of poetry are *Undiscovered Country* (Mother Tongue Publishing, 2018), *This Isn't the Apocalypse We Hoped For* (Caitlin Press, 2014), and *Understories* (Caitlin Press, 2010). He also has two chapbooks: *Four Neat Holes* and *The Picket Fence Diaries*. His poems have appeared in various journals including *The Malahat Review, GRAIN, CV2, Event,* and *Prairie Fire* as well as in anthologies such as *Heartwood, The Best Canadian Poetry in English,* and *Rocksalt*. Al Rempel currently lives in Prince George, where he teaches physics and science at a high school. He can be found at alrempel.com.

**Rebekah Rempel** studied creative writing at the University of Victoria. Her poems have appeared or are forthcoming in the anthologies *Refugium: Poems for the Pacific* (Caitlin Press), *Force Field: 77 Women Poets of British Columbia* (Mother Tongue Publishing), and *Unfurled: Collected Poetry from Northern BC Women* (Caitlin Press), as well as a number of journals and magazines. She has also contributed a poem to Bimblebox 153 Birds, which engages artists with the bird species that inhabit the Bimblebox Nature Refuge in Queensland, Australia. She lives near Dawson Creek, in northeastern BC.

**Harold Rhenisch** is the author of the critique of book culture, *The Art of Haying: A Journey to Iceland,* the sufic ghazals in "Two Minds," the spell craft of "The Spoken World" and twenty-seven other works of fiction, essays, poetry and environmental writing. He works as a professional editor in Vernon, and reviewer for the *Ormsby Review*. His *The Tree Whisperer,* an environmental poetics, is forthcoming from Gaspereau Press. For forty-five years, Rhenisch has worked on literatures of place from the grasslands east of the North Pacific.

**Dominique Russell** is the author of *Instructions for Dreamers* (Swimmers Group, 2018) and *Kensington, I Remember* (Russell Creek Press, 2013; 2016) and the editor of *Rape in Art Cinema* (Bloomsbury, 2010; 2012). Recent poetry can be seen at *carte blanche; Atlas and Alice* and *Cagibi*.

**Dennis Saddleman** was born in Merritt BC and raised on Coldwater Reserve. His life became a struggle when he went to Residential School in Kamloops, BC. He encountered drugs and alcohol which made his life dark and miserable. One day he saw the light, he's been clean and sober for 39 years. He became a creative writer. He has a passion for writing. From his family and friends, he earned the name, Word Warrior. His poetry took him all over British Columbia, Edmonton, Winnipeg, Ottawa, Toronto and Honolulu. Soon, he will publish a book of poetry and continue to gain recognition.

**Eleonore Schönmaier** is the author of the critically acclaimed collections *Dust Blown Side of the Journey, Wavelengths of Your Song,* and *Treading Fast Rivers* all from McGill-Queen's University Press. Her poetry has been set to music by Greek, Dutch, Scottish, American, and Canadian composers. She has won the Alfred G. Bailey Prize, the Earle Birney Prize, and the 2019 National Broadsheet Contest, among others. Her work is widely anthologized, and has been published in *Best Canadian Poetry.* As chair of the Barrens and Backlands group she worked to achieve the protected status of the Duncans Cove Nature Reserve. eleonoreschonmaier.com

**Christine Schrum** writes about the environment, the arts, relationships, and wellness from Victoria, BC. She's written about BC's beleaguered grizzly bears for *Smithsonian* and has interviewed David Barber, poetry editor at *The Atlantic,* for *The Writer.* Her poems have appeared in *CV2, EVENT,* and *A Verse Map of Vancouver* (Anvil Press, 2009), and her essays have been published in *Grain, The Rumpus, McSweeney's,* and other publications. In 2018, she was shortlisted for *The Malahat Review's* WordsThaw Prize.

**Jackie Seidel** is an Associate Professor of Curriculum and Learning at the University of Calgary. She is passionate about exploring the existential and pedagogical meanings of ecological and social justice issues with teachers, including biodiversity loss and climate change. She is learning Arabic, and enjoys writing poetry, knitting socks, and cycling. Several colonies of honey bees occupy her yard and she enjoys their sweet buzz, earthy scent, and putting her bare hands in the hives.

**Kelly Shepherd**'s second poetry collection, *Insomnia Bird: Edmonton Poems* (Thistledown Press, 2018) won the 2019 Robert Kroetsch City of Edmonton Book Prize, and was shortlisted for the 2019 Stephan G. Stephansson Award for Poetry. *Shift* (Thistledown, 2016) was longlisted for the Edmonton Public Library's People's Choice Award in 2017. Kelly has written seven poetry chapbooks, most recently *In the Space Between* (the Alfred Gustav Press, 2019). He is also poetry editor for the environmental philosophy journal *The Trumpeter*. Originally from Smithers, BC, Kelly lives in Edmonton, and teaches English and Communications at the Northern Alberta Institute of Technology.

**Bren Simmers** is the author of two books of poetry, *Night Gears* (Wolsak & Wynn, 2010) and *Hastings-Sunrise* (Nightwood Editions, 2015), which was a finalist for the City of Vancouver Book Award. *Pivot Point*, a non-fiction book about a wilderness canoe trip was published by Gaspereau in 2019. A lifelong west coaster, she recently moved to PEI.

**Christine Smart** grew up a farm in rural Quebec, studied, travelled and then settled on Salt Spring Island, BC, in 1989. Her book, *Decked and Dancing*, won the Acorn-Plantos Award in 2007. Hedgerow Press also published her poetry collection, *The White Crow*, in 2013. Her poems have been recently anthologized in *Refugium*, *Beyond Forgetting*, and *Love of the Salish Sea Islands*. She has been published in various literary journals. She also writes fiction and non-fiction. christinesmart.ca

**Kevin Spenst**, a Pushcart Poetry nominee, is the author of *Ignite, Jabbering with Bing Bong* (both with Anvil Press), and over a dozen chapbooks including *Pray Goodbye* (the Alfred Gustav Press), *Ward Notes* (the serif of nottingham), *Flip Flop Faces and Unexpurgated Lives* (JackPine Press), and most recently *Upend* (Frog Hollow Press: Dis/Ability series). He lives on unceded Coast Salish territory with the love of his life Shauna Kaendo.

**Susan Stenson**'s forthcoming poetry collection is called *At The Beginning of the World*. She lives in the Cowichan Valley with her husband, the novelist, Bill Stenson. Her work is widely anthologized, most recently in *GUSH* and *Refugium*. A celebrated creative writing teacher, Susan received a Prime Minister's Award for Educational Excellence in 2012 and has won several national prizes for her poetry, including The League of Canadian Poets National Poetry Competition.

**Rob Taylor** is the author of three poetry collections, including *The News* (Gaspereau Press, 2016), which was a finalist for the 2017 Dorothy Livesay Poetry Prize. Rob is also the editor of *What the Poets Are Doing: Canadian Poets in Conversation* (Nightwood Editions, 2018) and guest editor of *Best Canadian Poetry 2019* (Biblioasis). In 2015 Rob received the City of Vancouver's Mayor's Arts Award for the Literary Arts, as an emerging artist. He lives in Port Moody, BC with his family.

**John Terpstra** has published ten books of poetry and five creative non-fiction. He has won and been short-listed for a number of prizes. *Mischief* is his latest volume of poetry, and his most recent non-fiction work is called *Daylighting Chedoke*. One of his poems, *Giants*, is inscribed on a Bookmarks plaque that stands on the edge of the Niagara Escarpment, overlooking downtown Hamilton, where he also lives and works as a cabinetmaker and carpenter.

**Russell Thornton** is the author of *The Hundred Lives* (Quattro Books, 2014), shortlisted for the Griffin Poetry Prize, and *Birds, Metals, Stones & Rain* (2013), shortlisted for the Governor General's Award, the Raymond Souster Award, and the Dorothy Livesay BC Book Prize. His other titles include *The Fifth Window, A Tunisian Notebook, House Built of Rain, The Human Shore*, and his newest collection, *The Broken Face* (Harbour Publishing, 2018). He lives in North Vancouver.

**Kurt Trzcinski** is an ecologist that has studied many ecosystems around the world, and currently teaches ecology at the University of Victoria. He curated a poetry session at the 2018 International Ornithological Congress along with poets Stephen Collis and Lorna Crozier and launched a chapbook-anthology of science and poetry called *Migrations Songs*.

**Katherena Vermette** is a Métis writer from Treaty One territory, the heart of the Métis nation, Winnipeg, Manitoba, Canada. Her first book, *North End Love Songs* (The Muses Company) won the Governor General's Literary Award for Poetry. Her novel, *The Break* (House of Anansi), was bestseller in Canada and won multiple awards, including the 2017 Amazon.ca First Novel Award. *where* is from her second book of poetry, *river woman* (House of Anansi, 2018).

**Fred Wah** was born in Swift Current, Saskatchewan, in 1939, and he grew up in the West Kootenay region of British Columbia. Studying at UBC in the early 1960s, he was one of the founding editors of the poetry newsletter *TISH*. After graduate work with Robert Creeley at the University of New Mexico and with Charles Olson at SUNY, Buffalo, he returned to the Kootenays in the late 1960s, founding the writing program at DTUC before moving on to teach at the University of Calgary. A pioneer of online publishing, he has mentored a generation of some of the most exciting new voices in poetry today. Of his seventeen books of poetry, *is a door* received the BC Book Prize, *Waiting For Saskatchewan* received the Governor-General's Award and *So Far* was awarded the Stephanson Award for Poetry. *Diamond Grill*, a biofiction about hybridity and growing up in a small-town Chinese-Canadian café won the Howard O'Hagan Award for Short Fiction, and his collection of critical writing, *Faking It: Poetics and Hybridity*, received the Gabrielle Roy Prize. Wah was appointed to the Order of Canada in 2012. He served as Canada's Parliamentary Poet Laureate from 2011 to 2013. To learn more about his work, visit The Fred Wah Digital Archive at fredwah.ca.

**Emily Wall** is a Professor of English at the University of Alaska. She holds an MFA in poetry and her poems have been published in journals across the US and Canada, most recently in *Prairie Schooner* and *Alaska Quarterly Review*. She has been nominated for a Pushcart Prize and her most recent book, *Flame,* won the Minerva Rising chapbook prize. She has two books published with Salmon Poetry: *Liveaboard* and *Freshly Rooted.* Her next book, *Breaking Into Air: Birth Poems* is forthcoming from Red Hen Press. Emily lives and writes in Douglas, Alaska. She can be found online at www.emily-wall.com.

**Zachariah Wells** grew up beside a dammed stream in Hazel Grove, PEI. He now lives not far from a creek that drains Chocolate Lake into Halifax's Northwest Arm. He is the author of three poetry collections, most recently *Sum.*

**David Yerex Williamson** is a college instructor and poet living in northern Manitoba. His recent works have appeared in *Prairie Fire, The New Quarterly, Prairie Journal of Literature* and *Heartwood,* a League of Canadian Poets anthology in honour of our relationship with trees. David is an associate member of the League. When not teaching, writing or drawing, David shovels snow, cuts wood and chases his dogs along the historic Nelson River.

**Rita Wong** is the author of five books of poetry and an associate professor in the Faculty of Culture and Community at Emily Carr University of Art and Design on the unceded Coast Salish territories also known as Vancouver. She co-edited the anthology, *Downstream: Reimagining Water,* with Dorothy Christian.

Born under a water sign, **Cynthia Woodman Kerkham** has a degree from UBC in Asian Studies and English Literature. Her poetry has been published in most Canadian literary journals and has won awards, including the Federation of BC Writers and *The Malahat Review*'s Open Season Award. Her poem "Burnt Pot, Riverbank, Indifferent Sky" placed as one of five finalists for the CBC Poetry Prize. She has published one collection of poetry *Good Holding Ground* (Palimpsest Press) and co-edited *Poems from Planet Earth* (Leaf Press). She writes, edits and swims in Victoria, BC.

**Derk Wynand** has published eleven collections of poems, including his most recent, *Past Imperfect, Present Tense* (Bayeux Arts, 2010), a collection of fiction, *One Cook, Once Dreamin,* (Sono Nis, 1980), and several books translated from the German of H.C. Artmann, Erich Wolfgang Skwara and Dorothea Grünzweig. For thirty-five years, he taught English and Creative Writing at the University of Victoria, where he edited *The Malahat Review* from 1992 to 1998.

**Joe Zucchiatti** lives in Whitehorse, where he writes poetry and prose, helps manage the local liquor store, and practices increasingly goofy manoeuvres at the local skatepark, where he volunteers as an advocate and custodian. His writing has appeared in *Refugium, subTerrain* and *Arc,* among other magazines and anthologies.

# Notes and Ecologies of Poems

**Maleea Acker on "Hesitating Once to Feel Glory":** This poem was written, along with many others, on a small walkway just above the sandy shoreline of Lake Chapala, with the San Juan de Cosalá Mountains behind me. Lake Chapala, which sits at about 6000 feet above sea level, is Mexico's largest, and it is the epicentre of many watershed troubles in the country. Guadalajara and nearby towns use more and more of the lake's water; dams from Oaxaca empty vast quantities of invasive plant species into the lake, which then colonize its shores. The water levels rise and fall—when they are high, swing sets and wharves disappear; when it is low, farmers herd their livestock and build fences on the flats, which then lie in wait as hazards when the water rises once again. The fish many people pull from the lake are contaminated with mercury; childhood kidney failure is precipitously high in waterfront villages. Still, it is a beautiful place, the lake full with wildlife and the hills dotted with high altitude oak forests. Many in the Mexican community there have become my family.

**Solveig Adair on "grandmother river":** At the juncture of the Kalum and Skeena Rivers, on the unceded territory of the Tsimshian people, there is a small boat launch that touches both sets of waters. There is another river that joins the Skeena slightly upriver and the Skeena swells and spills with the joinings. Living at the edge of the river, cycles of water, of life and death, are as keenly felt as the pulse beneath our own skins. My grandmother taught me this and, shortly before her death, asked me to help bring her to the water that was such an integral part of her own history. Rivers are about connection. I have never forgotten my grandmother making her peace through her ties to the land and the water. This poem was born from the river that connected us, the pulse of arteries that drew us back again and again.

**Susan Alexander on "The Whirlwind...":** My poem was born of frustration. McNab Creek is one of only three salmon-bearing estuaries in Howe Sound/Atl'kitsem and home to bald eagles, Roosevelt Elk, and twenty-three species at risk. It supports birds, fish, amphibians and mammals. Its intertidal habitat sequesters carbon. The province ignored not just my voice, but protests from surrounding communities who spoke against Burnco's massive gravel mine project. Humans are blessed with memory and imagination, yet we don't clearly understand how our own lives depend on other life forms thriving. I'm fascinated by God's voice in the story of Job. God doesn't answer Job's understandably self-centred questions, but instead refocuses the narrative on the unfathomable diversity of the world beyond the human. Howe Sound is the stunning marine backyard of Vancouver. A recent rebound of marine life is delighting residents and visitors thanks to the extensive remediation of toxic industrial sites that leached poisons into the sound for decades. Think balls of herring and anchovy feeding salmon, sea lions, dolphins, orcas, and humpback whales. Yet, even as it revives, our province pushes again for re-industrialization. In addition to Burnco, a new liquefied natural gas (LNG) terminal will be built at the Woodfibre site near Squamish.

**Laura Apol on "Riven":** Here in Michigan, I live at the top of a steep ravine, through which flows a stream. The ravine and stream comprise a small part of the Muddy Creek watershed, which constitutes a small part of the Lower Maple River watershed, which forms a small part of the Grand River watershed. These collective watersheds drain into the Grand River and flow to Lake Michigan. Each October, freshwater salmon come from Lake Michigan, up the Grand River, to spawn in this little stream. Hundreds upon hundreds of them arrive to spawn and die. In my poem, I want to explore the paradox of this particular eco-geography, the watershed being both a separation and a coming-together: how the stream is part of larger systems of water, and the salmon are part of larger elements of ecology, their spawning at once both life-giving and death-making. There is a circular, cyclical quality to this watershed—a clear demarcation between downstream and upstream, past and future, life and death, and yet a simultaneous blurring of these boundaries, even as they are made.

**John Barton on "Palm Springs":** I have always been a water baby and a swimmer. In light of this, I read *Water: The Fate of Our Most Precious Resource* soon after Marq de Villiers won a Governor General's Literary Award for it in 1999. Having grown up on the prairies and in the watershed of the Bow River, I found those sections dealing with the world's driest regions most pertinent. Especially revealing was de Villiers' airing of how aquifers and rivers of the US Midwest were being drained and diverted to satisfy California's needs. On a planet where too many don't have enough potable water, swimming in chlorinated pools seemed a selfish luxury. Having now visited Palm Springs, California, I can say my poem's namesake is as beautiful and unsustainable as I'd visualized it to be two decades ago. "Palm Springs" begins with a question and, like a swimmer alternating strokes, glides through intermixing tropes: thirst, body, land, water, vitality, exhaustion, ageing, and decay. My swimmer's daydreaming. Are his semi-conscious imaginings a hallucination he'll shake off or a nightmare he'll wake up to after pulling himself from the pristine water he's so fortunate to be swimming through? Will he care?

**Gary Barwin on "The Birds, Butterflies and Snakes of Hamilton, Ontario":** As Wikipedia states: "Hamilton, Ontario's Cootes Paradise Marsh is a wetland at the western end of Lake Ontario, a National Historic Site, a Nationally Important Bird Area (IBA), and an Important Amphibian and Reptile Area (IMPARA)." It is also where the Chedoke Watershed, which begins above the Niagara Escarpment in Hamilton, arrives at the lake. Once an important navigational route, it has been the site of intensive work to restore it to its previously diverse and flourishing natural state, eliminating destructive invasive species such as carp. It is remarkable as a place in a city once known for its heavy industry where a wide variety of wildlife exists, from swans to eagles, blue herons to turtles. In the years that I have lived near Cootes, I have seen this very noticeable positive change and have been astounded to witness the biodiversity there.

**Lee Beavington on "Mountain Stream":** This poem is a collage of annual river walks I have undertaken with my father. We drive past Vedder Mountain Road in Chilliwack until the road begins to twist and undulate with the river. Leaving the logging road behind, we trek up the mountain stream, mossy stones serving the path. The Coastal Mountains birth such streams, coddled by grandmother conifers amid underfields of sword fern. Sometimes, the river is too wild to be walked. Or devil's club guards the banks. A choice arises: abandon the stream, or brave the rapids. The wilder option jolts the body full of adrenaline. Every footstep matters, every handhold the difference between safety and surrender. In this heightened state, with every sense strained, emerges an animal thrill. In becoming animal we become part of a deeper relationality. The temperate rainforest is no longer an object, a separation, an Other, but rather a breathing ecosystem that inhales and exhales with our human bodies.

**Barbara Black on "Dharana":** "Dharana" was painted by Canadian artist Frederick Varley in 1932. It depicts his lover Vera Weatherbie on the steps of his Lynn Valley house in what is now Lynn Headwaters Regional Park. Lynn Creek Watershed, located in North Vancouver, BC, spans an area of 55.2 kilometres. It is bordered by Seymour River and Mosquito Creek watersheds, originates in the protected Lynn Headwaters Regional Park and discharges into Burrard Inlet. At lower elevations, it encompasses heavy residential and industrial areas which have contributed to the complete loss of estuary due to ongoing urban development. Still, the stunning alpine and riparian scenery draw a steady stream of both locals and visitors to this area year after year. Those, like me, who grew up close to the wildness of Lynn Creek Watershed feel that, no matter if we move far away from its creeks and rainforest, its stunning beauty remains a part of us and we will fiercely protect it for generations to come.

**Nicholas Bradley on "Provincial Letter":** In the increasingly busy city of Victoria, where I live, it's easy to feel disconnected from the mountains, glaciers, and rivers of central Vancouver Island. "Provincial Letter" comes from my time as an appreciative traveller in the Comox Valley, where, when the snows melt—as on a warm day in February—the sense of being immersed in a liquid landscape is powerfully disorienting. As rivers run down to the Strait of Georgia, they might remind urban visitors that for all our summer chatter about watering restrictions and dead lawns, our part of the world is defined not only by drought, and by the salt water that surrounds us, but also by the fresh water that shapes and reshapes the land. In "The River of Rivers in Connecticut," Wallace Stevens wrote of "The river that flows nowhere, like a sea." Yes—and I think of rivers in our houses, flowing back and forth, joining us and going nowhere.

**Kate Braid on "Water to Water":** Maybe because I'm a Pisces, I love swimming, but I love water anywhere : in pool, in stream, in ocean, even in the living room fish tank—though lately with the floods in the East, I've tempered that a bit. I grew up on the Prairie but after almost fifty years of living on the west coast, I don't think I could ever again live away from ocean. There's deep peace in looking out over water, even during storms.

**Terri Brandmueller on "Green Rain":** "Green Rain" borrows its title and the phrase "long veils of green rain" from the great imagist poet Dorothy Livesay's poem of the same name. These images were in my mind's eye one day as I was enjoying feeding the ducks in Stanley Park's Lost Lagoon. It was raining and dreary but the ducks were noisy, greedy, and full of life and colour. I looked over at the Bayshore Inn and suddenly remembered an odd story about reclusive billionaire Howard Hughes camping out in the hotel during the early '70s. Rumours were rife, but he was apparently on the run from the US tax authorities and he and his entourage stayed for six months, taking up the top four floors of the hotel. The piece of this story that always stuck with me was that it was reported that in the entire six months he never left his room, and standing there feeding the ducks that day, I couldn't resist relocating Hughes to the Stanley Park watershed.

**Brian Brett on "Beautiful Boys":** I was born for water. A wounded child, I retreated to water, and have spent most of my young life near water, gazing, swimming, wading, drinking it. The waters of my world. I drank from so many of the rivers and lakes in western Canada by the time I was thirty I can no longer count them. I drank from the river where I fished steelhead, and leaning over the side of the boat in our largest lakes while trolling for the giant Kamloops lake trout. I swam like a frog with

221

an awkward grace, a grace I didn't know on land. I never feared drowning. Now I fear for water, the vast poisoning of our liquid planet, and the infecting of all water everywhere. Acid rain poisoning our unreachable alpine lakes. The inevitably toxic mines. I'm told all the creeks, every one I drank from in my childhood, are contaminated with Beaver Fever. My generation did this and our terrible gift to our children is the duty to give these waters back to the living, so that the future children of the world will be able to leap once again into the waters of life.

**Michelle Poirier Brown on "The Weight of Snow":** The rivers I know best, whose forces and rhythms I have studied, are the mountain rivers of British Columbia. For 15 years, I worked as a government negotiator, trying to find solutions to problems affecting people whose lives depend on rivers altered by hydro development. I negotiated, as well, with Indigenous people whose connection to their river has been similarly dislocated by colonialism. I can relate cubic metres of water to megawatts of power, understand the relationship between the snowpack on the northern Coast Mountains and the sustainability of 20 percent of the commercial sockeye catch in the mouth of the Fraser. Yet for this call to write about our connection to watershed, my tongue hung limp in my mouth. Because I was not formed in the mountains. I am a prairie girl, with a deep connection to the Red River of the Manitoba Métis homeland. There is a bend in that slow, brown river as familiar to me as my own ribcage. I needed to return to the watershed of my childhood, the flat, fertile, lacustrine plain left behind when the Laurentide Ice Sheet collapsed about 9,500 years ago, and Lake Agassiz drainage pushed salt water over the Bosporus.

**Jenna Butler on "excerpt from *Magnetic North...*":** The two pieces included in the anthology were written while I was living aboard a tall ship in the archipelago of Svalbard during the summer of 2014, documenting the changing Norwegian Arctic. While I was on the Antigua, I found myself writing along the links between threatened polar regions and the great boreal forest I call home in northern Alberta. Just as the Arctic sea ice was melting faster than ever before, and the glaciers were calving constantly through the strangely warm summer, the boreal forest back home was tinder dry and moving into a new cycle of catastrophic fires. Although I was half a world away, the connections between northern Norway and Canada were clear: the temperatures were rising, and both land and ocean were shifting rapidly as a result.

**Claire Caldwell on "Sounds a River Makes":** The Yukon and Klondike rivers are the soundtrack to this poem, which I wrote during my residency at the Berton House in Dawson City, in summer 2016. Dawson sits at the confluence of these two rivers, and the town's perimeter is hemmed on one side by their banks. I lived in Whitehorse as a kid, but I've spent most of my life in big cities. That summer, I often felt overwhelmed by the scale and beauty of the Yukon landscape—and by a strange kind of emotional whiplash at returning to this site of childhood memories. But rivers, with their changing cadences and shifting banks, have a way of tugging you back into the present. So I got to listening, and found out just how much the Klondike and Yukon had to say.

**Trevor Carolan on "Elaho":** The poem was inspired by a Squamish First Nations medicine walk with my wife and children in the rugged Elaho River country north of Squamish led by Cease Wyss and the late John Clarke. We camped along the river, then trucked next morning through apocalyptic clear-cut logging action before entering serious old growth territory where Cease gave practical explanations of the traditional Coast Salish healing plants that flourish there. Climbing higher, we arrived in wonderment at a tiny meadow rich in tall grass and delicate valerian flowers. John told us that aging grizzlies frequent these pockets searching for the valerian root that eases their arthritis. Knowing you're in a grizzly bear's local hangout clicks on an extraordinary state of mindfulness.

**Terry Ann Carter on "from watershed to watershed":** After reading an article on the way that beaver homes (lodges) store millions of gallons of water underground in wetland "sponges" that surround beaver colonies, ultimately benefiting many fish, birds, amphibians, plants and people that make up the ecosystem, I decided that the small quiet haiku might pay homage to this work.

**Karen Charleson on "earth other's birth tears":** A recent photo shows our daughter, holding her own young daughter, on the beach here at Ayyi'saqh. Underneath this picture, our daughter has written: "We are part of these lands and waters forever." Our family has deep roots in Hesquiat Harbour, in the traditional territories of the Hesquiaht First Nation, in the territories of the House of Kinquashtakumtlth. My husband puts it quite succinctly. He says: "This is where we belong." The creek that runs alongside our home, is the lifeblood of the Ayyi'saqh watershed. It is born in the mountain valley above and behind us. Its waters rush, meander, wind and twist and cascade their way through old growth forest and ravaged clearcuts, to reach the flat lands nearest the ocean shoreline. It is from here that we most often watch the creek, as it makes its final push to merge with the sea. I wrote this haiku as a description, a tribute, and a celebration, of the creek here at Ayyi'saqh, and the watershed of life that it supports.

**Karen Chester on "Estuarine":** I have a dog, more fox than wolf I'd say. Last winter I took an ekphrastic poetry workshop and chose two images that felt like they would inspire words: both photos, both Wolf. Being a bit beach-obsessed myself I placed one wolf on the shore (the photo made me feel the salty wet of his legs), the other in the heavens (the amber orb of her eye made her seem other-worldly). And so began the conversation. The art that inspired: *The Lost Wolf* and *The Rain Wolves*—both by April Bencze.

**Daniel Cowper on "Thirst":** On Bowen Island, in Howe Sound, a cold snap interrupts our monotonous rainy season with a brief period of intense dryness. Arctic outflow pushes away rain clouds which would otherwise move in from the warm ocean to pile up on our mountains. The cold air is very dry, and sublimates moisture from the soil, just as it chaps lips. Sub-zero temperatures crystallize and concentrate the remaining surface moisture into ice. The products of this freezing and sublimation can be chthonic, like dirty frost-jacks puffing up the dry skin of the ground, or exquisite, like the fine, silvery follicles of ice extruded through the pores of fallen branches. Water begins to sink through the suddenly-sandy earth into the rock below. Streams vanish underground. Depressions that have held pools of rainwater ever since the end of summer freeze over, and suddenly drain: stiff ice-coverings left behind are lined with a diminishing series of silhouettes. This drought creates a strange, euphoric atmosphere in the forests, and marks in many ways the climax of the famine season of winter for local wildlife.

**xavier o. datura on "genius loci":** Imagine a developer—corpulent, dressed in a designer suit, with slick hair and a wearable phone—accompanied by a scourge of lawyers—representing some corporate cement conglomerate—submit an application to extract a quarter million tonnes of rock per year from sacred Mount Sinai. Or raze a portion of the Garden of Gethsemane in Jerusalem for luxury housing? Or construct a gravel quarry on the site where the Kaaba—considered by Muslims to be the "House of God"—currently resides. Not only would this proposition be preposterous, but genuinely offensive—quite literally sacrilegious. And yet this is precisely what has come to pass on "Sheridan Hill" (Sam'e:ent in Halq'eméylem) in S'ólh Téméxw—the traditional watershed of the Stó:lō. This colonial desecration is all the more offensive when one recognizes that Sam'e:ent is sacred to the Katzie First Nation in particular, as it is their site of Creation— their Garden of Eden, if you will (although the analog is not perfect). I composed this poem while conducting place-based research at the Maple Ridge Environmental School after a student asked me if the Katzie First Nation creation story was "real"?

**Wendy Donawa on "Stone's Deep Accord, its Steady Presence":** I drafted this poem one chilly October while resident at one of the Banff Centre's wonderful poetry programs. I wrote in something of a fugue state, gazing at the slope rising from the valley below, its aspens blazing gold in the late afternoon light, its textured screes, gullies, elk pastures, clouds surging, light shifting, and snow possible at any moment. My brief dwelling in the short darkening afternoon seemed a blip in the valley's millennia, its compressions and upheavals, its fossils and erosions, its glaciers and waterways, its enormity of time.

**Daniela Elza on "Our Own Lemon Creek":** In 2013 a large tanker carrying jet fuel for forestry helicopters battling summer blazes dumped approximately 33,000 litres of jet fuel A1 into the waters of Slocan Valley's Lemon Creek. The road was a narrow decommissioned logging road closed to traffic due to slides and crumbling banks. The driver proceeded up Lemon Creek Road, past two signs that said the road was closed. The swift-flowing Lemon Creek pours into the Slocan River downstream of the spill (*The Tyee*, Aug. 7, 2013). That same year my husband and I separated. After twenty years the ecology of our relationship had incrementally eroded, had become a precarious habit. Did not sustain us anymore. My mind rationalized it, but it took a long time for my body to understand this slippage, this unravelling. The future too—a road that keeps narrowing. We are bypassing the chorus of warning signs telling us to turn around. We're the waters of Lemon Creek, the smoke from the fires, the twenty rusty cedars they chopped behind my house this Spring. We are this fragile, this pollutable, this irreplaceable. "Do you think there is anything not attached by its unbreakable cord to everything else?" asks Mary Oliver (*Upstream*). We know now, this cord isn't unbreakable.

**Dorothy Field on "Sleeping with the River":** In the 1890s, the young City of Victoria began to culvert and pave over its rivers and creeks—a health measure. Waterways had become dumping grounds and cholera sources. But the creeks are still there below. Put your ear to the manhole covers. Listen. The Rock Bay Creek Revival is a group working to daylight "Rock Bay Creek" since its Indigenous name has long been lost. It rises in my neighbourhood, Fernwood, and flows into the Gorge. We've created art signs to wake the neighbours to the creek below. Those with wet basements are already aware. We will never bring back the hills clad with Garry oak, cedar, and Douglas fir, the gurgling water that poured over the rocks, the shellfish along the shore, frogs and salamanders, spring camas turning the fields blue, pink shooting stars and chocolate lilies gazing out to sea. But the eagles still soar overhead. Maybe kids will again dip hands to catch the sparkles. And maybe, we will again see herring in the eelgrass, coho in the creek. Many thanks to the Esquimalt and Songhees Nations who have consulted on the signs' imagery and wording and taught us so much about connecting to the land.

**Heather Fraser on "Respawn":** I started writing "Respawn" while cleaning out a clogged shower drain. It was a revealing moment for me, seeing and touching the remains of what I'd washed down the drain every day. I couldn't pretend that the drain was a magic vanishing system that removed my refuse from existence. It was all still there, clumping together and transforming the ecosystem in ways I hadn't tried to understand. This was especially alarming to me as a resident of Greater Victoria, where our wastewater flows directly into the Juan de Fuca strait.

**Art Fredeen on "old engravings":** I live part-time on the shores of Lake Ontario in the east end of Toronto. Lake Ontario is a constant source of inspiration to me, its complexion and mood changing by the minute. This particular haiku was written in mid-February of 2018, a year when many bays in the greater Toronto area froze over. This ice accumulates the weathering, scars and cracks of an entire winter, reminding me of engravings on an old silver tray.

**Rhonda Ganz on "Catching Rain in a Paper Bag":** Losing part of our natural world feels as strong to me sometimes as the loss of a person much loved. In grief we adapt or die. I remember spring puddles in the field next to my urban elementary school teeming with tadpoles—don't think I've seen a single tadpole in the past twenty years. I didn't start out to weave the story of water into one more personal, or vice versa, but in my experience, poems don't take well to being planned. This was one of the first poems I wrote after my father died.

**Kim Goldberg on "Skein":** I live in downtown Nanaimo, in a cottage leftover from the coal-mining days, beside the Millstone River where pink and chum salmon still spawn. Noisy flocks of Canada geese wake me on winter mornings as they overfly my house to feed at the estuary. I walk the river's edge upstream, moving ever deeper into dark pleats of cedar and Douglas-fir. All the way to Deadman Falls—impassable for the coho, so a side channel with carefully sculpted pools and gravel and shade trees was engineered for their spawning. I have always been drawn to pantoums, to their spooky magic of creating two parallel narratives by recycling words and images. The writing of a pantoum is like a mad scientist's experiment. You never really know what the result of the poem's repetitions and juxtapositions will be. The salmon and forests and geese are one narrative. But how does that narrative change when the human element enters the poem? And what is the endgame of this intertwining? These are the questions I set out to explore in "Skein."

**Ariel Gordon on "Excerpt from *TreeTalk: Winnipeg*":** On July 29 & 30, 2017, I sat on the Tallest Poppy's patio—less than 500 meters from the banks of the Assiniboine—as part of a Synonym Art Consultation residency in Winnipeg. I spent the weekend looking up into the boulevard elm and writing snippets of poems which I hung from the boulevard tree using paper and string. Passersby were invited to TreeTalk too. That June, Winnipeg's street trees were hosts to: cankerworm, elm spanworm, and tent caterpillars. Which meant worms dangling from trees on silky lines, almost completely covering the sides of buildings. Some people called it The Year of the Caterpillar. Other people dubbed it Wormmageddon. To humans, it was unpleasant. But to the trees—their deep roots accessing groundwater, caressing the sewage pipes—the worms constituted a health hazard. The worst-hit trees had their leaves eaten down to the stem. This defoliation can push trees into their death spiral, because growing a new set of leaves uses up energy they'd otherwise use to survive the effects of climate change—heat waves, drought, superstorms—on top of the usual challenges of pollution, soil compaction, and mechanical damage. The research out there says that most cities are relying on street trees to mitigate climate changes, so we have to figure out how to keep them healthy.

**Alisa Gordaneer on "Flying River":** This poem crept up on me, like an unexpected but welcome rainstorm. It is an erasure poem from an article I was reading in *The Atlantic* magazine, by Gabriel Popkin. The title of the article is "Trees Could Change the Climate More than Scientists Thought," and I became fascinated with the idea of trees actually being behind the weather. There was a poem behind that idea, I felt, so I looked immediately behind it, trying to sort out the forest from the trees by taking away the bracken of prose. The result is this poem, which to me represents an obvious truth that was there all along, if only we could just take the time to see, and could be said to be written by Popkin as much as by myself.

**Laurie D. Graham on "Antler River":** The river has been given a few names: Deshkan Ziibi, Askunesippi, La Tranche, the Thames River. The city—London, Ontario—that was ordered to form around it by John Graves Simcoe did so reluctantly and with difficulty. Now the forks are the perceived geographical centre of London, and all of life congregates there on your average day, as well as the building-up and the tailings and the detritus. "Antler River" tries to capture all this on an atypical day in February, the temperature suddenly in the double digits, the ice melted, water high and silty, the parkas flung off, relief and alarm comingling. And the ways that the built-up erodes and overpowers what's there has led to this weird warm day in what should be the depths of winter, and yet the forks still contain their selfhood, their sacredness, in spite of that smothering.

**Marlene Grand Maître on "Her Voice a Forge":** The writing process for this poem began with a startling image. While riding a bus, I thought I saw a woman on the sidewalk cupping a bald doll's head in her left palm. I will never know what she was really carrying, but that image was so charged that I immediately recorded it in my notebook, As soon as I got home, I started writing. Like a magnet, the image attracted a polyglot prophet, Vancouver Island watersheds, their parched rivers and streams, and the melting Yukon glacier that caused the Slims River's overnight change of direction. May the lament of the watersheds, and of all the species that depend on them, pierce us.

**Raine Gutierrez on "I am the Sweet Water":** My science class was discussing (at the time I wrote my poem) the effects of climate change on the environment and I thought it would be cool if I touched on that. I wrote from the perspective of the water to add a more personal touch and create something easier for the readers to connect with. I thought if the water was a person, it would be fun to play around with the water and its relationships. I started with the osprey and thought it would be neat to write about the relationships getting progressively worse like climate change.

**gillian harding-russell on "Bypass Project":** I wrote "Bypass Project" while the Regina bypass was being built to ever extending deadlines and costs. Unfortunately, this project designed to assist economic progress carries a downside in that it removes the original prairie vegetation and leaves the soil vulnerable to the arid and windy environment. So not only are prairie songbirds threatened by the reduction of grasslands habitat but they may also be affected by the loud construction machinery. Last spring 2018, I listened with interest to a biologist interviewed on CBC who had noted how the Savannah Sparrow in these construction sites had learned to adapt its call to a shriller piping in order to be heard over the roar of engines and heavy equipment. A hopeful evolutionary development for a brave species in a difficult plight.

**Maureen Scott Harris on "Groundwater 2":** The city of Toronto sprawls across three major watersheds, the Humber, the Don, and the Rouge. I live within the Don River watershed at the top of the shoreline of Lake Ontario's precursor, glacial Lake Iroquois, but my poem originated in the Rouge River watershed and an earlier poem, "Groundwater." In October 2016 I participated in Abundance, a harvest celebration of the Pickering Lands, calling attention to the agricultural potential of class A farmlands, expropriated in the 1970s for an airport never built, and still in the limbo of federal ownership. The notion of a second airport had again raised its ugly head, and the celebration was a form of protest using vocabularies of dance, poetry, and food to nurture a vision of relationship with the lands vastly different from the one proposed by various local politicians and developers. My poem explored groundwater as an image for a barely-conscious yearning for renewed connection to the earth. "Groundwater 2," published here, embraces groundwater as female strategist: model against despair; practice for undermining the larger culture's refusal to acknowledge our destructive behaviour towards the land, and the need for reparation.

**Richard Harrison on "Under Western Water: Returning to Work":** The Western Water is the Alberta Flood of 2013 that ran from Eastern Rocky waterways all the way down to the South Saskatchewan River. My house filled when the Bow flowed up the storm drains along its banks, water lifting things in the house and toppling them into silty water that dried like paint; in this way the Flood also took things it didn't drown or break. As I write this, people are working hard to prevent the effects of another flood, and The Bow is calm, but changed, as all the rivers were, and all the landscapes around them. It is filled with millions of river stones that form islands in its middle, altering the current. There are sheer walls where there used to be sloping banks and trees. There's a small white-water rapid where there used to be smooth water. Kayakers and surfers take turns piloting themselves into this rapid and staying there as long as they can. The difference between the Great Alberta Flood and just another June was three extra days of rain that fell here because the air masses that normally move north stayed put. Calgary is built along its river banks; up close you learn that on the basis of even small changes in the atmosphere, huge consequences come.

**Diana Hayes on "Walk to the Wetlands":** From sunroom windows on Salt Spring Island, looking through dense stands of hemlock and cedar, I catch blue reflections off Little Stevens Lake situated in the 100+ acre tract of wetlands, streams and twin lakes that form an S-curve of wild and ever-changing beauty. The lakes are classified as eutrophic with marginal sources of potable water due to excessive growth of algae and the resulting oxygen depletion. A seasonal creek runs through my forested acreage, feeding the winter marsh and flooding the lower stretch where shoulder-height sedges, cattails and reed canary grasses flourish. A riparian ecosystem now protected by the Islands Trust, this area attracts many species of flora and fauna including songbirds, raptors and waterfowl. We have found evidence of beaver and river otter, as well as the endangered trillium lilies. My neighbour reports seeing three white swans. In early spring the chorus of frogs is deafening. In later summer, after persistent drought and extreme fire risk, the edges of the marsh are lost to brittle dryness. We've identified seven species of bats with sonic detectors from our deck. At night, barred and great horned owls strike up raucous vocals. Although their flights are truly silent, their presence is welcome.

**Steven Heighton on "Lost Waterfalls":** Some years ago, the Kingston poet Eric Folsom, while doing research on the Cataraqui River and its tributaries, found a two-century old reference to a waterfall north of Kingston, east of the Perth Road—a waterfall that no one has been able to locate since. Of course, waterfalls can be seasonal. For example, every spring in the Little Cataraqui Conservation Area, just north of Kingston, a vigorous and permanent-looking waterfall, maybe thirty feet high, appears for a few weeks and then vanishes for the rest of the year. Could that be the one the explorers saw? Possibly, but there must be many other seasonal falls in the region. At any rate, the melancholy metaphor of a vanished cataract appealed to me (back when I found melancholy irresistible, because I hadn't yet experienced enough of it in my life) and the poem wrote itself, as they say.

**Iain Higgins on "Small Song for the Watershed":** Around the time I was first learning about "the hydrologic cycle" in elementary school, I was happily spending my after-school hours wandering creek-beds that have long since vanished under the concrete and asphalt of urban and suburban sprawl—though some of them are now being freed again in a process called daylighting. Crayfish were common in those creeks, as was household waste—old fridges and stoves, in particular. This use of creeks as covert dumps was no doubt one reason why cities and municipalities decided to bury them alive, confining them in pipes and culverts, even though the dumpers were behaving with impeccable capitalist logic: outsource whatever costs and consequences you can. As a kid I had no more idea of economic systems than I did of natural systems, so my wandering and wading were thoughtless pleasures. The capitalist and scientific mythologies (that is, the foundational, orienting stories) that ordered my life were detached from my lived experience. To achieve that detachment, the white Euro-American culture to which I was heir, had had to bury its own ancient streams of thought that it might now be worth rediscovering (in the literal sense). Hence this translation, which celebrates a living world of natural equals centred on sharing water.

**Bruce Hunter on "Two O'clock Creek":** 2 O'clock Creek as it was originally spelled is the meltwater from Wilson's Glacier, part of the rapidly-shrinking Columbia Icefields that straddles the Great Divide of the Canadian Rockies between Alberta and British Columbia. Located just east of Saskatchewan Crossing in Banff National Park, the creek crosses the Kootenay Plains and empties into the Upper North Saskatchewan River. The Kootenay Plains is named for the Kutenai people who came to this sacred place on a high mountain prairie to celebrate, hunt and trade with the Plains Cree among others for more than 5000 years.

**Maureen Hynes on "High Water Mark":** The poem was written for one of the "Poetry Walks" that a group of Toronto poets have been giving with the Lost Rivers Toronto organization (lostrivers.ca), which aims to highlight the city's intimate connection to its water systems by tracing the courses of forgotten streams. The Humber River, however, is not a "lost" river—it is one of Toronto's two major rivers, and its main branch runs for about 100 kilometres from the Niagara Escarpment, joins with the East Humber to flow into Lake Ontario. The Humber River collects from about 750 creeks and streams and tributaries in a fan-shaped area north of Toronto.

**Ishtar on "Animal to Water, 2005":** I have spent much of my adult life lying alone in unhealthy apartments, trapped by Myalgic Encephalomyelitis, depression, PTSD and MCS, poverty and lack of supports. For me, lake swimming and hiking are powerful, medicinal, nervous system resets. But because I can't see shore or where trails are, I need sighted people's assistance, which I can rarely get, in order to access these wild places I yearn for. I hurt a lot because of not having this help and not being able to access these healing places I need. This poem is based on an experience I had in 2005 where, after pushing through ableism and sexism, I was free to focus on swimming because I found someone to direct me to shore when I was done. In the water I felt released from the grip of illness and trauma, freed from barriers imposed against my abilities and from limitations clamped down on me, connected to my animal self and the lake as entity. For this time, immersed in what I needed, I had back what seemed lost. I felt powerful, bigger than isms, micro-aggressions and sighted, male surveillance; that I belonged both in that place and to myself.

**M.W. Jaeggle on "Ubi Sunt":** The beginnings to this poem emerged while aimlessly picking at a tuft of sedge on an August day several kilometres from the Horsefly River, a salmon carrying river which, by way of Quesnel Lake and the Quesnel River, drains into the Fraser River. If this poem can be said to portray some of the life within the Fraser River Basin, it's because it was given to the senses. This poem is thereby beholden to this region.

**Beth Kope on "Call it Wild Swimming":** A lake swim celebrates our rich wealth of clean waters, connects our bodies and souls with that natural world and motivates us to protect our lakes. I have many favourite lakes and each has a unique character. But Pease Lake, a tiny jewel in the northern Highlands, is exquisite. I love it for its soft water and the magical hours I've spent on its shores and in its waters. Pease Lake is contained within its own watershed. Pease Creek flows into the lake from the south and then out from the lake on the southeast shore on into McKenzie Bight in Saanich Inlet. Only 3.8 hectares in size and at its deepest 6 metres, most of the shoreline is older second growth forest. The lake is part of Mount Work Regional Park to the east and Gowlland Tod Provincial Park to the west. Cutthroat trout are present in this watershed and the Canadian waterweed (*Elodea canadensis*) has been a problem at times in Pease Lake. The water quality is good, and there is one small public access point which helps limit our human impact.

**Alyse Knorr on "Swamp Preserve":** I wrote this poem during an artist residency in Florida at the Big Cypress National Preserve, a freshwater swamp ecosystem just north of the Everglades. Founded in the 1960s as the nation's first national preserve, the Big Cypress Watershed is home to a rich diversity of flora and fauna, including many endangered species such as the Florida panther and sandhill crane. My poem references two plants that fascinated me during my two weeks at the Preserve— the ghost iris and the strangler fig. The ghost iris, or *Iris albispiritus*, is a mysterious and rare white iris long thought to have disappeared but existing now in freshwater Florida ecosystems. The strangler fig is a very common type of vine that wraps itself around a host tree, often to the point of killing the host.

**Elee Kraljii Gardiner on "Exorcise":** During the fall I set myself a rule, as an off-page writing prompt, to hike a tiny bit of the Baden-Powell Trail in North Vancouver every week. The gift of the hike was as much for the interest in ritual as for my mental health. News of misogynous laws and violence against women was taking a toll: every day I heard about acid attacks, rapes, bodies, abuse. A friend's neighbourhood was being clear-cut for condos and the carnage and displacement was painful, linked to other repressions and destructions. My daughter had just moved across the country for college and I was missing her, feeling angry about what might befall her and be called "legal", so as I hiked I listened to her favourite album and let endorphins wash the rage, and rain wash the tears, and mist wash the sweat. Coming to the pivot point of the hike, Quarry Rock, and looking over the enormous vista of deep fjords, the beauty of the Tsleil-Waututh land was a relief. I took to pausing on my run to absorb the sound of the creeks tumbling down the hill. The reminder of cycles became a promise of endurance, and connection.

**Aaron Kreuter on "Hydrophobia":** Hydrophobia is a very real condition. One of the side effects of rabies, it leads to an irrational fear of water. What a perfect way—I thought when I first encountered the condition—to explore the human relationship with water in all its wonder and horror. So, line by line, sentence by sentence, image by image, the poem came to be. The earth is water; we are water. Yet, at the same time, we are killing the earth's waterways. We must rethink our relationship to the lakes, rivers, aquifers, oceans, and toilet bowls that surround and sustain us, and we must do it soon, or that last bureaucrat dumping that last load of poison into the last river will have won. "Hydrophobia" is an attempt to think through these sobering facts. I wrote this on the shore of Lake Kahshe, in late August.

**Anita Lahey on "Don River, Crossings and Expeditions":** In 2014, while living in Toronto, I immersed myself in "the urban wilderness." I signed up for "nature babies" and hiked the High Park woods with my infant son. A neighbour and I enrolled in a continuing education course that consisted of weekly—lengthy!—bird-watching hikes. And I was, by some wondrous chance, invited to participate in a poetry-infused version of a Lost Rivers Walk. These popular walks acquaint people with the city's buried (and troubled) watershed. In preparation, participating poets were treated to an informative meander down the long-beleaguered Don River, led by Lost Rivers maven Helen Mills and longtime Take Back the Don organizer John Wilson. They brought the Don's burgeoning restoration, its grimy industrial past, and its far deeper Indigenous-agricultural legacy, to life. I was stunned to realize how little attention I'd previously paid to this powerful waterway that cuts through Toronto, and through which runs so much of the city's history, for better or worse. This poem was first published on *NewPoetry* in April, 2015, and later in the Gesture Press chapbook, *Reading the Don.*

**Fiona Tinwei Lam on "Lost Stream":** Connaught Park and the adjoining Kitsilano Community Centre are a few blocks away from where I live. Year after year, large sections of the park that are used as playing fields for rugby, soccer, baseball and cricket are fenced off to be "remediated" only to be "remediated" again. When it rains hard, water accumulates on both West 12th and West 10th Avenues bordering the park: pedestrians get sprayed by passing cars; sidewalks are covered with puddles; the grass becomes sodden. Around the park's circumference, a number of old trees have fallen. When I first saw a map of Vancouver's old streams and saw that that a large stream or creek used to exist running diagonally across where Connaught park is now, it all made sense. It's as if the waterlogged park has been telling us all along that it wants to return to its original state! One of my neighbours who has lived in our neighbourhood for over fifty years told me that people used to go fishing in the various streams in our area until they gradually were all paved over for housing.

**Zoë Landale on "Bute Inlet":** This poem comes from a solitary wilderness adventure I undertook twenty years ago. Bute Inlet, a dramatic milky green, is one on the principal inlets of the BC coast. It is located in the unceded territory of the Comox Nation. Wikipedia says Bute Inlet is "one of the most scenic waterways in the world." The mountains there rise sheer from the sea, some close to 10,000 feet. A old friend from commercial fishing days got me the loan of a falling-down cabin. The area is home to many grizzlies, black bears, and all five species of salmon. My family was fiercely opposed to me going there (grizzlies!) and was convinced I'd come home in a body bag. Bute is fed by the Homathko and Southgate rivers, which drain the Homathko Icefield, one of the largest icefields in the southern half of the Coast Mountains. I was blown away by the size and beauty of the Homathko river; I could hear it roar half a mile away from my cabin. All five species of salmon spawn in the Homathko; it is the closest to the pre-settler abundance I've encountered on the coast.

**Joanna Lilley on "Desert Fish":** The poem is about the tecopa pupfish, a tiny creature who lived in two particular hot springs of the Amargosa River in Death Valley, California, and nowhere else. As the hot springs became increasingly popular with humans, the pools were enlarged and the water flowing from them diverted. As a result, the water became too hot for the pupfish to survive and by 1970 or so the species was extinct. I came across the Tecopa pupfish while I was researching a book of poems I was writing about extinct species. I wanted to make sure I wrote about many different species, not just famous extinctions such as the mammoth and dodo. I felt compelled to write about the pupfish because I am intrigued by any species who lives in water, as I feel so at home in water too, and also because of the way we caused its extinction. I often walk around three ponds in the forest where I live and always wish they were deep enough and devoid of mud enough for me to swim in. What species would I be guilty of harming or eradicating if my wish came true?

**D.A. Lockhart on "Dull Thuds over Waabiishkiigo Gchigami":** Pelee Island is everything. Stretched out along the side of the Pelee Islander II, she rises from the waters of Waabiishkiigo Gchigami, this inland freshwater sea named for the people of the deer. When you arrive you arrive at the federal dock at Westview and this island is everything. Surrounded by the shallows of the lake settlers call Erie, this is the most southern inhabited portion of land in our northern country. It is an island of drained marshes, of transformed land, and an southern Carolinian ecosystem that beats on in spite of the change. Today, it holds on despite threats of record lake levels, algae blooms, and fish fly swarms. It rests on the curtain seam of the America border. At forty-two square kilometres it is a sizeable piece of real estate. Famous for wine, monarchs, and healthy bird populations, it does struggle to hold its two hundred plus full-time residents. For half of the year, like the Three-Fires ancestors, me and mine hold up on our portion of alvar in a ocean of bird in a tipi we own. Our goal to preserve and sway in the medicine of this island. Poems and other lyric works arise from this portion of creation for me. I know that it is protected by that great underwater panther and protector Mishibijiw. A timeless part of creation that we often watch lap by Fish Point, patrolling the space between islands above hundreds of shipwrecks. This is the world I want to and need to reflect.

**Christine Lowther on "Not the Lake":** To live beside a creek that never dries up even in drought is an opportunity for profound gratitude. It's also mysterious and awe-inspiring. More recently through the driest five months I've witnessed in Clayoquot Sound during my twenty-seven years here, I experience anxious relief after a blessing of rain that raises the creek's voice just a little higher. This is un-ceded Tla-o-qui-aht territory of Wah-na-jus—Hilth-hoo-is Tribal Park, an island that would have been clearcut if not for blockades presented by Indigenous and non-Indigenous residents together. All the streams in the ancient temperate rainfor-est amaze and delight me, as they emerge from the mystery of this singular forest on this precious planet. They come "out of nowhere" … gifts from life to life.

**Tanis MacDonald on "A Feminist Guide to Reservoirs":** I live on the Grand Riv-er Watershed, on the traditional territory of the Haudenosaunee and Anishnaabe peoples, on land that was, via the Haldimand Treaty of 1784, bequeathed to the people of Six Nations for their service to the British government in the Revolution-ary War. In 2019, the city of Waterloo was ranked the most dangerous Canadian city for women to live in by the Canadian Centre for Policy Alternatives. I come from Winnipeg, long known as the violent crime capital of Canada. The Laurel Creek Watershed is located in the centre of the Grand River Watershed, covers about 74.4 square kilometres and includes tributaries of seven other creeks. I walk in or around the Laurel Creek Reservoir every week, and think about what walking in a wild but urban space means to my feminist practice and what feminism has to do with land listening and decolonization.

**Dan MacIsaac on "American Bullfrog":** American bullfrogs are overrunning the watershed habitat of frogs native to land west of the Rockies. This bombastic amphib-ian's competitive strategy includes eating its smaller, less aggressive cousins. Like some politicians and corporate raiders from south of the border, this cold-blooded creature is not at all quiet about the takeover. Its tweets blare and blast.

**Adelia MacWilliam on "Lost Lake":** Lost Lake was inspired by conversations I had with Gary Snyder's literary executor Mark Gonnerman in the Lost Lake Café in Seattle while we were attending a poetics retreat held by Paul Nelson. Mark and I were both staying in the Subud House on Capitol Hill and would go there for coffee in the morning. Mark, who wrote a book about Gary Snyder's *Mountain and Rivers Without End*, founded the Aurora Forum at Stanford, which featured guest speakers, including the Dalai Lama, with whom he had the incident at the airport!!! Lao Tzu is in the poem, because Snyder's landscape poetry, as David Hinton writes, is "indistinguishable from the Tao," where is no duality between the "Wild" and the civilized. The café served as a remarkable backdrop for these conversations. I wrote it as a lake experiencing a fracturing of identity, a kind of psychogenic fugue, which speaks to the erasure/alteration of bodies of water by urbanization. However, I also wanted to include my experience of "no duality" with several worlds overlapping. After all, I was in the café with Mark having conversations about Snyder, who Hinton considers to be the third great eco-poet following Jeffers and Rexroth.

**Murray Mann on "The Lost Land":** In 1949 the BC government gave the Aluminum company of Canada, Alcan, the rights to the water, timber, and minerals that fell within the Ootsa Lake reservoir, or the upper Nechako watershed. On 8 October 1952, Alcan closed the gates of the diversion tunnel and began the flooding of a northern wilderness. The reservoir Alcan built is 235 km in length and covers approximately 92,000 hectares (890 square kilometres) over much of what was traditional Cheslatta territory. The Nechako river was shut off completely for four years; and then, when the reservoir was finally filled, Alcan opened the gates of the Skinslake spillway, changing a seasonal creek of about 5 cubic meters of water-per-second flow into a stream of 500 cubic meters of water-per-second flow. This seasonal creek, however, passed right through the traditional villages of about 200 Cheslatta people. They were given ten days notice to leave the area. Rio Tinto Alcan still controls the waters and the flow of the Nechako, and they still produce aluminum at their Kitimat smelter. My fascination with the social and ecological horror of this story comes both from my own astonishing ignorance and from its startling history that continues to this day.

**David Martin on "Homecoming":** In the summer of 2018, I took a trip to visit the Athabasca glacier, in Jasper National Park. While there, I began to think about something I had learned from a geology course: there are legacy pollutants trapped within glaciers across the globe, and as glaciers melt these pollutants, which we believe to be safely part of the past, will re-enter our watersheds. Our chemical history will be coming back to haunt us.

**Ilona Martonfi on "Chernobyl Evacuee's Lament, Kopachi Village":** *Wormwood ... the waters became wormwood; and many men died of the waters, because they were made bitter.* Revelation 8:10-11. Write. Write it Kateryna. Full frame camera with a wide angle lens under a crescent gibbous moon. Write. A search for the faces of the disappeared. A group here, and another there. Write. They bought black handkerchiefs. Buried them in sealed zinc caskets under cement tiles. Chernobyl on the Pripyat River, 140 kilometres north of Kiev. They didn't know it back then, no one said anything about radiation. It was on a Saturday, April 26, 1986. No. 4 reactor blew up and caught fire. Write. What if we washed the floors? they asked. Bleached the wood stove? All, so we could come back. Be close to our family graves. Write Kateryna. The moon wakes the grey wolf's dream. Radiocesium trapped in clay. The Dead Zone.

**Rhona McAdam on "By the Glass":** This poem was long in the making. It took shape after talking to someone who had been teaching overseas for many years. She said she couldn't get over the fact that Canadians flush their toilets with drinking water. This has become a kind of watery mantra for me. But I had been anxious about water for years, since the limitations of the water table were explained to me in Grade 11 Geography class: we are at eventual risk of losing our supply of drinking water. Yet culturally, still, the penny does not drop. Restaurant diners take a sip or simply leave those complimentary water glasses untouched. Half-drunk cups of coffee or tea circle our drains. A Native Plants workshop advised: "your toilet is not a garbage can", and "leaving the tap running while brushing your teeth wastes enough drinking water to fill a local swimming pool". We drain ancient aquifers to fill plastic water bottles, swimming pools, ice rinks. The leaking taps and toilets we don't get around to fixing. Those thirsty ornamental plants in our gardens with needs well beyond our local precipitation. Car washes. Lawns. Fracking. And of course toilets, flushed with precious drinking water.

**Wendy McGrath on "Kilrane":** Kilrane was inspired by a stay in southeast Ireland at the home of my husband's uncle. We could walk along a short path to the sea and to the beach where it was cold, windy, and utterly deserted. Once on the beach I was struck with a sense of the unfamiliar, in an otherworldly landscape of splayed seaweed, shells, and rocks—a tableau that defied the earthly. Clouds and sea battered against each other, moved by the strength of some great unseen force. There was a warning to be heeded. I felt a strange sadness and fear on this lonely stretch of shore—that this seemingly indestructible, perfect balance would change. The poem, "Kilrane" was my attempt to hold on to this moment, this place—to become part of the sea and believe that it, and I, could be infinite and immortal.

**Lorin Medley on "Kus-kus-sum":** Kus-kus-sum is the name given to the abandoned Fields Sawmill site in Courtenay, BC. K'ómox First Nation and Project Watershed are working to purchase and restore the site to its natural habitat. Kus-

kus-sum the poem was written under the influence of Alice Notley's "The Descent of Alette," a feminist epic poem with a hypnotic cadence that, for me, evoked the image of riding a bicycle through circular time. I cycled the road from Comox to Courtenay as a nineteen-year-old, past the eagle tree on the K'ómoks First Nation, ancient intertidal fish traps, and a bustling Fields Sawmill. At sixty-one, I cycle the same road. From the pedestrian walkway on the 17th Street bridge, I watch seals pick off juvenile salmon trapped against the unforgiving steel retaining wall along the river bank and imagine my future self looking down at sloping banks and native grasses.

**kjmunro on "lake visit":** Memories of an A-frame cabin on Canim Lake in the Cariboo... paddling through the summers of my youth in a canoe close to shore, swimming, fishing, lying on the dock listening to lapping waves... & a recent visit— sitting in the dark around a crackling campfire, sparks flying up into the night air, across the lake from that cabin, remembering my father & his love of birds, & the sign he made for this place—"Walden Too"...

**Ulrike Narwani on "Godsend":** I still have visions of the beach at Maya Bay on Ko Phi Phi Leh, an island off the west coast of Thailand, see the white sand slide into lucent water, their shades of brilliant light merging. The cry of seagulls the only sound. At the end of the 20th century this environment was still pristine, peaceful, and bountiful, schools of fish easily visible in the clear water. In 2004, a massive earthquake in the Indian Ocean triggered a tsunami that devastated many of the islands in the Phi Phi chain. Some of these islands experienced a tsunami drawback, saw the water in their bays suddenly recede as if sucked into a giant hole leaving hundreds of fish stranded on wet sand. An unexpected boon for many. This drawback was a strange, impossible phenomenon, the natural order seemingly reversed. People stood in shock and disbelief. Most were unaware of the immense wave heading towards them. In "Godsend" this tsunami springboards into a metaphorical one—the rising wave of aberrant heat looming over our planet, a threat that is pushing fragile watersheds, and their bounty on which so much of life depends, to the brink of destruction.

**Lorri Neilsen Glenn on "Yellow Deck Chair...":** My ancestors, both maternal and paternal, lived and worked on water—in Scotland and Ireland, on Hudson Bay, in Métis communities on the Red River and later on the North and South Saskatchewan. Now I live by the immense and fierce Atlantic, a daily reminder of the power, persistence and mystery of water. Parts of this coast are eroding steadily, and storm surges are higher and more frequent than they once were. A 2019 Environment and

Climate Change Canada report predicts Atlantic Canada's sea levels will rise by 75-100 centimetres by 2100. Flooding will quadruple in frequency by 2050. Hurricanes are a constant threat. Each year we hear fewer songbirds, and yesterday I saw beavers building at the edge of a lake threatened by the encroaching ocean. Salt is poison to the animals.

**Thos Nesbitt on "Childhood Danford Lake":** Danford Lake is a lake of two kilometers in Quebec. It sits at the head of a string of lakes that flows into the Picanoc River, the Gatineau and the Ottawa. Ecology is the study of relationships. Who or what is the person who, through many years, peered into Danford Lake? Or the person who comes now to read these words? Poetry can arise from meditation, the awareness that we are, that is always present, right here, but never known. When we become aware of the mystery we are living right now, we have a choice. We can just be—aware-ing being—a moment, for a time complete, open, changing, and without any other "result". Alternatively, we can turn, opening ourselves to words that might suggest: The watching world/ Unfolding, silent,/ Leaf-like/ Here. Poetry can then sometimes emerge. Such poems, and these words of explanation, are not themselves true or valuable. But they have value if they can point a way to the wonder-ing from which they—and "Childhood: Danford Lake"—arose. This moment, ourselves, the poem: all unfathomable.

**Charlie Neyelle and Thos Nesbitt on "Water Heart":** Sahtu is the eighth largest lake in the world and the last of the world's relatively pristine, vast lakes. It remains extraordinarily clear, due (among other factors) to its extremely low year-round temperatures, its relatively low biological productivity, and its relatively plankton-free waters. The watershed has a high degree of ecological integrity. It is "healthy" from the perspective of the Elders, and it sustains the community of Déline. As suggested in the poem, the Elders see the lake as alive and sustaining the entire watershed. Much of the watershed is now protected from industrial development, due to the inclusion, in the Sahtu Land Use Plan, of much of the *Water Heart: A Management Plan for Great Bear Lake and its Watershed*. In 2016, UNESCO, together with Déline authorities, designated the lake and its watershed as Tsa Tué Biosphere Reserve. At 9,331,300 hectares, Tsa Tué is the largest biosphere reserve in North America.

**Geoffrey Nilson on "The Sound of Cellulose":** North Surrey in the 1980s curated neighbourhoods with bird names instead of streets, the same tree at the foot of each driveway. Thousands of middle-aged men selling networks of asphalt that spiraled out from the shopping centre like sinkholes. Kids turned loose and free to roam across all acres until the sun came down. On foot. But better, on bicycle. Powerline right-of-way criss-crossing field and park: Green Timbers; Tynehead; Invergarry. The bicycle = freedom. And it takes you places, first experiences of forest. Something more than the sound of metal and the body, of sprockets and the rain slapping wet on bark and the sleeves of your jacket. A silence which is also song. The bicycle takes you far away from the place you learned its power, but never leaves, faithful frame under yours, a foundation to build on. The poem happens when you stop thinking about the poem, when your muscles at attention strain through the trail bliss of rock earth as you find safe passage over roots and loam. The line is the cadence of the wheel as you push forward, until the revolutions stop, finally, for good.

**Emily Olsen on "Herring Season, 1992":** As observed in a remote town in Haíl-zaqv Territory.

**Catherine Owen on "You Make Me Ache River…":** My watershed is the Fraser River, the longest river in BC, near which I have lived at various times of my life. "You make me ache river" was written when I was living on the Vancouver side of the water near where the White Pine Canadian Mill had been torn down and where, soon, an entirely new village of condos and stores would be built. Grieving the death of my partner, I spent much time watching the river in its contradictions of industry and seemingly still-pure beauties. Realizing how, in the end, we are all helpless to truly alter fate, I took solace in how the river just "gets on with it," never subsiding into any final paralysis of sorrow but persisting in endless forms of eco-logical creation, despite.

**Nancy Pagh on "Drift":** Lately I have been working on a series of poems inspired by a beautiful little antique booklet called "The Barnacles of British Columbia." I believe I discovered this treasure at a used book shop in Port Alberni in the 1980s while on a field trip to the Bamfield Marine Station. The soft charcoal drawings, blue jacket, and lovely descriptions of barnacles remind me very much of a poetry chap-book—even though this is a scientific publication. I am generating poems about things I "hold on" to—a nod to the barnacle's ability to attach itself to rocks, hulls, and whales. I generate each poem by making a list of interesting or "key" words and phrases from the field guide, then incorporate many of them into the draft. "Drift" began with the entry for *Lepas anatifera* Linnaeus: the pelagic gooseneck barnacle. The key words were: length, goose, enclosed, body, striated, absent, series of square, scattered, young, interspaces, driftwood, along the coast. This is a memory of swim lessons at Skyline Marina in Anacortes, Washington, when I was about five years old. I hated them.

**Arleen Paré on "Anthropocene":** I wrote this poem between two worlds, two selves, which is where I find myself these days: the world/self that presents the end of life as we know it, and the world/self that can't bear to see it. So I focus on the tree, one tree. In this way I can manage. A pin point of existence. Maybe that's how we have always managed, most of us.

**John Pass on "Fish Ladder":** "Fish Ladder" is from a collection, *Water Stair*, of multi-dimensional river poems. Its immediate geography is the salmon-rich watersheds of the Fraser and Stikine rivers. Its cultural context is the psychology and aesthetics of our simultaneous push and resistance toward source, destination. The poem contrasts Indigenous and Western European attitudes and is especially critical of the latter, but both provide instances of the capacity of our desires and technologies to interrupt acceptance of our place in landscape, of tragic pride and default to superstition. *Water Stair* was published in 2000 and shortlisted for the Governor General's Award in 2001. In the context of the book "Fish Ladder" falls between the poems "Hiker Ascendant At Mountain Creek" and "Adam's River".

**Jeremy Pataky on "Falling Scene":** I write from one of our last intact watersheds. I eat its salmon, drink its water, and celebrate it even as its glaciers recede. Meltwater from one forms McCarthy Creek, which flows by bearing too much silt to drink. So I drink Clear Creek—a tributary—unfiltered. Downstream, McCarthy Creek flows into the Kennicott River, which joins the braided Nizina, one of many that flow into the Chitina, a Copper River tributary. The Copper (or Ahtna River, named for the area's Athabascan people) empties into the Pacific through a massive delta. I built my home far upstream, planting roots even as nearby permafrost melt causes land to slump and slide. Forests burn in all-time high temperatures. Backyard ice melt contributes to rising seas. The longer I stay, the less remote, the more linked to the globe this place feels. I fill my jugs with the creek and hear news about lead-poisoned kids damaged by tap water. I catch rain while others are lawbreakers for doing so. I sleep by an open window inside one of my wild watershed's headwater songs. In dreams, it sounds like a dirge for so much gone, a raga braced for loss.

**Barbara Pelman on "Blueberry Creek":** The poem recalls a time when I lived in the Kootenays, with the Columbia River on my left and the little creek on my right. Evenings I would fall asleep to the sound of creek noises and mornings walked its banks through salal and cottonwood. It was only through research that I found out about habitat loss as the community grew and, like me then, lived carelessly without knowing and protecting its watershed. In the days of living by the creek, and having a garden with peach trees and blueberries and corn, I was not at all ecologically aware or a warrior for the earth, but this was 1970 and I was more tuned to feminist issues, to educational battles, to self-growth. It takes many years to realize how interconnected all these issues are, and how equally important it is to pay attention to the cutthroat trout struggling in the culverts of Blueberry Creek as it is to pay attention to the dynamics between women and men. Not either/or but both/and. It was wonderful to return to that time, living by the creek and listening to the river, and connecting to Hopkins ode to wilderness—long live it yet.

**Kirsten Pendreigh on "Planetary Hubris":** This poem began as a flippant exploration of geoengineering, but it reared up and surprised me with its underlying emotional heaviness. I heard Anna-Maria Tremonti interview an astrophysicist proposing a massive geoengineering project to cool the Arctic. The plan called for 10 million wind-powered pumps to pull up cold sea water and form more surface ice. The absurdity of that 10 million number seemed to underscore a paradox: a system based on unquestioned calculations of limitless economic growth is the very reason our planet is at the brink of disaster. I began researching other climate mitigation ideas and wondering about their unintended consequences. Humans (settlers) are confident they can master nature, but history is rife with their failures. I do cling to the hope that scientific ingenuity will play a part in finding a solution to the climate crisis; I can't yet accept the alternative. However, we have to start with massive carbon emission reductions—we can't just buy time with laboratory-simulated mitigation projects that could surprise us in the real world.

**David Pimm on "Watershed Sonnet":** Blepharitis is an inflammation of the eyelids (the inner eyelid makes moist contact with the eye and causes problems with the oil glands; there are often flakes or crusts near the roots of the eyelashes). And a stye is a small abscess on the eyelid and an infection at the root of an eyelash. Combine them in a single eye and, I felt, as in so many other contemporary settings, here is a watershed with pollution issues. Using 'watershed' as a metaphor for the fluid actions beneath an eyelid flowing over the surface of an eye involves, reveals and highlights aspects both of watersheds and of eyes. For our bodies have watersheds, whether inside or out. Reciprocally, we can see the world as an animate body, one that can get infected and struggle to function. Lastly, the sonnet: this name comes from the Italian *sonnetto*, literally a 'small sound' or a 'small song'. Such poems originally were composed with strict iambic pentameter rhythm and a characteristic pattern of end rhymes (not least the type called Shakespearean: 3x4+2 lines). My poem may once have contained some of these elements, but alas the eye-fluid of this particular poem has washed them awry.

**Pamela Porter on "Peace Country":** This suite of poems emerged in the early summer of 2012, as my husband, son and I set out on a road trip, which took the unusual route of driving north toward the Peace River Valley before turning east toward the prairies. Arriving at Hudson's Hope, we got out of the car and walked around the Bennett Dam. Still somewhat new to Canada, I'd spent the previous decade and a half raising children and paid little attention to the subject of dams or to their contentious histories. We made a second stop in the valley where the bucolic Peace River wound through fields thick with grass already being cut and baled, fields of canola in bright yellow bloom, while eagles soared in the blue overhead. The experience would change me forever. I sent an email to Patrick Lane telling of our visit to the Peace, and he replied with his ongoing grief over the canyon now drowned by the Bennett dam. The poems arrived almost seamlessly, mostly when I was lucky enough to sit in the back seat, generally undisturbed. Read Sarah Cox's book, *Breaching the Peace,* if you want to get really angry at the injustice of it all.

**Marion Quednau on "Whether Report":** My poem derived from a sense of loss in witnessing the changes during my 30-year stint living on a ridge above the Fraser River. The wetlands directly below my farm were barely saved among incoming industrial parks and highway expansions, and fewer dairy farms were surviving along the valley's river basin. There are horses in my poem because my own, often rescued from desperate situations, grew shrill with the incoming weather changes, "up on their toes" with thunderstorms in winter, and crazed hailstorms in summer. "What next?" they seemed to say as they sought shelter. The lines came to me in one fell swoop, but I let the poem rest to discover what it meant. I'm not a speculative fiction fan, but it seemed this poem might be of similar ilk. I had imagined a mutated world of extremes, old creatures returned, rusted landscapes. And I wondered of the people who "dwelled" (it seemed a more ancient/fragile word) in nature, altered its former beauty and abundance. I dreamt these dwellers returned to an original wonder or spirituality, with first tongues, a world wherein they no longer fancied themselves entitled or in control, but humbled, chastened. A cruel new beginning.

**Brent Raycroft on "Blueroof":** The Depot Creek Nature Reserve is a 72 acre property that has been tended and protected for more than 40 years by artist Kim Ondaatje, and was purchased by the Land Conservancy of Kingston Frontenac Lennox & Addington in 2013. Blueroof is the name of Kim's home, which has a blue roof, but by extension it is the name of the local geography as well. The stream is Depot Creek, a tributary in the Napanee River watershed, which leads from the lakes north of Bellrock down to Lake Ontario. The scenery is not dramatic here where the shield meets the limestone plain, though the hills are modestly rolling. You need to follow trails like those blazed on this nature reserve to see the small-scale grandeur of the place. Settlers in this part of Ontario were both French and English, and many names are bilingual portmanteaus. Depot Creek, surprisingly, is from "deep eau" rather than "depot." Similarly the town of Bellrock. When I showed Kim my poem she reminded me that "Blue Roof" was a single word—no longer spelled Bleuroof, but part of this same phenomenon.

**D.C. Reid on "I Could Simply Give In":** I am the one person in a hundred who spends fifty or more days alone in the back country of Vancouver Island. My life has always been about water. In this case, in a January snowstorm, while fly fishing the Taylor River west of Port Alberni, I noticed black shapes passing through my legs and serpentining around my boots. When I looked closely, I was in a school of a thousand sockeye salmon, living on in winter, a time when they should have been long gone. Sockeye begin entering the Somass River, en route to the Taylor, in late May. Stragglers in the middle of winter are rare. Like this, some of the peak experiences of my life have occurred alone on rivers and the land, including bear, cougar, wolves, elk and canyons where I may have exceeded my chances of returning unharmed. In forests all over the Island lie calcium vertebrae of salmon. Cedar trees receive 14 percent of their carbon from carcasses toted into the forest by bears. I am happy to move from one medium to another.

**Al Rempel on "Tillted South":** About three years ago, our family moved back to the Buckhorn, a rural area just southeast of Prince George, and awash with reminders of the last ice age. It is thought that the whole area was once under a giant lake that drained towards what is now Summit Lake on the watershed divide north of Prince George. Approximately 10,000 years ago this lake was plugged at its southern end by a late surge of glacial ice and rocky debris. When the lake suddenly burst southwards it carved out the Fraser river and canyon, eventually emptying its load into the delta we see now near Vancouver. My daughter & I routinely go to the small stream by our place, to see what it is doing, and we stand on the rocks pried from glacial till, wondering what stories they tell. Because of the forest fires that burned around us in recent years, testimony to these uncertain times of climate change, we constantly monitor the moisture levels of the forest using the stream as our indicator. When the forest dries, the stream disappears under the gravel. To stand in the stream and study the rocks is a to read a kind of origin story: the intersection of past & future, of sky & earth, a story navigated by the gravitational compass of upstream & downstream.

**Harold Rhenisch on "The Promise of Rivers Shanty":** This poem celebrates my fifteen years on the Chilcotin Basalt. It was written to extend Red Lillard's farewell anthem to the lost rivers of British Columbia. I wrote it to complete *Motherstone: British Columbia's Volcanic Plateau*, which the photographer Chris Harris and I made together in 2010. The poem complements the map of rivers draining from the shield volcanoes of the Chilcotin that Chris drew for me. For four years, I had written poems about salmon going to sea, which won second prize in the CBC Poetry contest in 2005 as "Catching a Snare Drum at the Fraser's Mouth." That year, I followed the salmon to Campbell River on Vancouver Island. After the four years on saltwater, in 2009 I travelled with the salmon up the Columbia River, from Astoria to my home valley, the Similkameen. A long sequence, *The Salmon Shanties*, followed, and my return with the salmon of N'kmp to our home in syilx territory. A new version of my *Motherstone* poem, now called "The Promise of Rivers Shanty," is among them. In this full form, it holds the rivers of both the Fraser and Columbia Basalts, where salmon and prickly pear cactus meet.

**Dominique Russell on "Russell Creek":** I live in a city of buried rivers. Early Torontonians polluted their waterways, then cemented them over, making way for housing. Choosing the cheapest solution has a long history in this city. It's such a strange thing, to bury a river. It not only deprives us of the beauty rivers bring to cities, it deprives us of an understanding of nature and time. The only reminders of what was lost comes to us as inconvenience: dents and curves in our roads, and flooding, as the rivers rise. Close to my house there is a creek buried in 1876. Suffocating it was seen as the solution to a cholera outbreak. It's named for an unsavoury city official who shares my last name: Russell Creek. Unlike the Garrison or other buried rivers, Russell Creek left no impression on the city's consciousness. It fascinates me nevertheless, this ghost creek, and my sense of loss for something I have never known, as a tiny microcosm of ecological grief; a love we didn't know we had for things that disappear before we even know they're there.

**Dennis Saddleman on "Water is Life or Death":** On my healing journey, they told me water is life. They told me, before I was born, I was submerged in water for nine months in my mommy's womb and that's every sacred. They told me after I die, someone in my family will wash my body with sacred water and dip fir boughs in water to brush me off. It's getting my body clean and I return to earth. In 2002, in my community, there was an election for chief and council. I was elected a band councilor. Our community had issues with water. We had concerns about our river, it was on the list for being an endangered river because the water was low and it affected different species of fish. Federal Government wants to build another pipeline through our community, and we are concerned about our drinking water which is an underground aquifer. I think about my grandfather. Many times, he would go to the river and pray for water everywhere. He told me water is precious. He told me talk to the water spirits, they will listen because they are our relatives. I have learned water has very strong power and I have learned to respect the water, for water is life or death.

**Eleonore Schönmaier on "-40C":** I was born and raised in the Red Lake district of northwestern Ontario which is part of the Hudson's Bay watershed and is the setting for -40oC. Despite the severity of the climate my father was almost fully self-sustaining. He had a large vegetable garden and collected berries from the bush. Even though he lived in a settlement with no public transportation and no grocery store he refused to own a car. He traveled only on foot, on skis or by bike. On his last day, November 25, he had cycled the ten kilometres into town to buy a liter of milk. The Ojibway artist Patrick Hunter created a banner in honour of my father showing him cycling through the forest. A woman said to me that my father "showed us what is possible."

**Christine Schrum on "The Last Lake Sturgeon":** We've all seen the heartbreaking photos of whales and sea turtles that have consumed plastic bags, but the creatures in our Great Lakes struggle, too. Researchers at the University of Toronto recently found microplastics (particles five millimetres and smaller) in nearly all the fish they tested. Lake Sturgeon weren't named specifically, but I chose to write about them because conservation pieces often highlight more conventionally charismatic animals. These fish are certainly impressive in their own right; the largest one on record was ten feet long and weighed more than four hundred pounds. The Committee on the Status of Endangered Wildlife in Canada currently lists Lake Sturgeon as "threatened," largely as a result of dams and historic overfishing. But microplastics, including the microbeads found in many body-care products, pose an insidious threat as well. Every time we brush our teeth, we impact our watersheds. As Dr. Jane Goodall says, "You cannot get through a single day without having an impact on the world around you. What you do makes a difference, and you have to decide what kind of difference you want to make."

**Jackie Seidel on "Post-Concussion Syndrome, or; The Impacts of Protest":** Originating in snow and glacier melt in the Rocky Mountains and foothills west of Calgary, Alberta, the Ghost River flows through the traditional territories of the people of Treaty 7 including the Blackfoot Confederacy, the Tsuut'ina First Nation, and the Stoney Nakoda First Nation. The City of Calgary is also home to Métis Nation of Alberta, Region III. This watershed covers nearly 1000 square kilometres. The Ghost flows into the Bow River which meets the Elbow River in Calgary. The traditional Blackfoot name for the city of Calgary, where the two rivers meet, is Moh'kins'tsis. This watershed is the major source of drinking and irrigation water for the drought-prone communities of southern Alberta. From 2015 to 2017 the expansive spruce forests of the Ghost River region were subject to extensive clearcutting. This is the story for large sections of the eastern slopes of the Rocky Mountains. The missing forests and bare slopes were a contributing factor to the destructive and extensive flooding in southern Alberta in 2013, as the land was unable to absorb the massive amount of snowmelt caused by days of unprecedented heavy rains.

**Kelly Shepherd on "This Poem is One Pillar":** The city of Edmonton is uniquely situated on aspen parkland, the transitional zone between prairie grassland and boreal forest, as well as on the North Saskatchewan River. Edmonton is the northernmost large city in North America, and its proximity to Alberta's oil sands makes it an important industrial and political location. "This Poem is One Pillar" is part of a larger work that explores the city's geography and shadow geography, its natural and built environments, and the often unseen or unnoticed relationships between the city's various inhabitants. In this particular poem, these inhabitants include (among others) public transit passengers, American elm trees, and rainclouds.

**Bren Simmers on "Judd Beach":** Along the banks of the Squamish River, Judd Beach is located in Brackendale, BC. Fed by four wild rivers (the Elaho, Cheekeye, Cheakamus, and Mamquam), the Squamish eventually empties into Howe Sound. This watershed supports salmon runs of pink, chum, coho, chinook, and steelhead that black bears and overwintering eagles feast on. Carcasses dragged into the forest return nitrogen to the soil, the trees shade the salmon fry, and the cycle continues unbroken. For several years, I lived a short walk from Judd Beach and visited its trails through all seasons. In this poem I sought to recreate the experience of that place. To stand on the shore, watching the fast-flowing glacial water make its way towards the ocean. To create a sense of current in the text, displacing the lines, offering different ways of reading the river.

**Christine Smart on "Wild Place":** Nothing was truly wild on our farm in Quebec except for the creek that burbled and snaked through the gulley. Nature befriended me by that creek: the sound of water running over smooth stones, damp air on my cheeks and birdsong in red maples overhead. Away from people, noise and demands, I could hide and be myself. The farm, as I knew it, no longer exists. It was a mixed farm with a variety of crops, animals and eggs. The farmhouse, barns, chicken houses and machine sheds were demolished so tractors could run through the yard and plant corn in straight rows. No chickens, no rhubarb, no vegetable garden. Does the creek still run wild and free? In my mind's eye, this part of the watershed for the Ottawa River has dried up or been polluted, after the red maples were cut and the land drained and ploughed. More fertilizers and pesticides were added for corn. No frogs, no birds, no wetland for minnows, bugs and birds. In the seventies and eighties, small family farms couldn't survive with larger government quotas and markets demanding high tech milkers and storage tanks. A larger scale farmer bought our farm for monoculture.

**Kevin Spenst on "In the Time of Particulates":** In 2011, I had a poem in "The Enpipe Line: 70,000 km of poetry written in resistance to the Northern Gateway pipeline proposal." Initially a blog curated by poet Christine Leclerc, the print version was launched outside the Vancouver offices of Enbridge, where celebration doubled as protest. Years later, due to resistance on many fronts, most notably under the pressure of Indigenous communities, the pipeline was nixed by the federal government. These days, pipelines are back in the headlines and the struggle continues, not only to prevent environmentally disastrous projects from seeing the light of day or the darkness of the earth, but to also raise a broader awareness. Two summers ago, forest fires from British Columbia's interior blotted out the sun over the Lower Mainland. The italicized lines from the poem "In the Time of Particulates" came to me while cycling home from work. For the rest of the poem, I imagined my way into a camping trip near a watershed. It's now happily found its home in this anthology, which is part of a wider debate that will profoundly affect future generations. With the power to raise awareness in words, poets have the potential to alter how actions are perceived. For saving the planet is not radical. It's an essential celebration of what we can be together.

**Susan Stenson on "Amniotic":** The Cowichan Valley has three rivers: The Chemainus, Cowichan and Koksilah, as well as lakes, estuaries, ponds, streams and creeks, each sensitive ecosystems. I was writing this poem in the fall of 2018, a dry fall, everyone worried about the salmon returning to ground too dry to spawn. Water wasn't rushing in the creeks in autumn and that silence was deafening. All I could think of was water is shedding its skin. A scene from the film, *The Miracle Worker*, where Helen Keller speaks her first word, *water*, kept wanting into the poem which seems fitting for the silent lack of understanding a watershed's importance to life on the planet.

**Rob Taylor on "Weather in Dublin":** This is a true story, recorded as it happened. As a writer who has lived most of his life in a temperate rain forest, "language" and "water," as concepts, feel interchangeable (ditto "poetry" and "storms"). Words, like drops of water, pool together magnetically, irresistibly. They gather and gather, and what manifests out of all that gathering can destroy or salve, or do both. It's a miracle we often don't appreciate until it's gone.

**John Terpstra on "A Brief History of Settlement on Hamilton Mountain, from 1789":** My research into and writing about Chedoke Creek dovetailed with a request from the painter, Petra Zantingh, who was building her "Trees of the Book", a collection of 52 paintings based on the occurrence of trees in the Bible. She assigned me Exodus 15:27: *Then they came to Elim, where there were twelve springs and seventy palm trees, and they camped there near the water.* The verse is part of a larger story of refugees on the hunt for a new home, and the ongoing need for water. I thought of the Michael and Charity Hess family, and their friends: ten adults and forty children, plus cattle and other animals, forced from their homes and making the trek from Pennsylvania to the western end of Lake Ontario, after the American Revolutionary War. There are other dislocations involved in this story, of course, but the settlers chose the Niagara Escarpment and built *Spring Farm* at the source for Chedoke Creek. The creek now runs in storm drain pipes beneath the streets of a suburban landscape, as invisible and vital as the copper-tubed creeks which water our homes and support our daily lives.

**Kurt Trzcinski on "Pitcher Plant":** Pitcher plants have fascinated biologists for centuries prompting the question: What are the evolutionary forces that led to such an amazing and unique adaptation? Carnivory in plants is an extraordinary example of convergent evolution; it has evolved many times in distantly related taxonomic groups to solve a very important problem—acquiring nutrients in nutrient-poor environments. Pitcher plants evolved a leaf structure that folded upon itself such that it formed a pitcher-like structure that could hold water. Many pitcher plants also have evolved scents, sugars, and waxes to attract prey, which then slip and fall into the fluid held by the pitcher. Several families of pitcher plants also have evolved digestive enzymes to help promote decomposition of the prey and the subsequent incorporation of nutrients. An interesting array of aquatic organisms have co-evolved to live in association with pitcher plants. These aquatic organisms live part of their life-cycle (unharmed) in the pitcher-plant's aquatic ecosystem—many species of which can live and reproduce only inside a pitcher plant. This micro-world teems with beauty, and mystery.

**Emily Wall on "If this was the Euphrates":** I lived on a sailboat for four years on the Fraser River in Vancouver, B.C. The Fraser is often considered a major "traffic" river with big barges and a large shipping lane. But it's also an ecologically rich river.

We docked our boat on small marina up the river from Steveston, tucked behind a little island. The river there was especially rich for bird life: eagles, herons, mallard ducks, and swans all lived there on the water. One of my favourite aspects of living on the dock was the deep intimacy with bird life on a daily basis. The mallards in particular spent a lot of time on the edge of the river and even on the dock. One year a mallard pair laid their eggs in one of my garden pots, and everyone living on the dock had the joy of watching those eggs hatch into baby ducklings. Sleeping over fish, waking to eagles, and spending my days watching ducks float right by my feet was such a beautiful way to live in this watershed.

**Zachariah Wells on "The Pond":** The creek/pond that this poem is about belongs to the Trout River watershed in Central Queen's County, Prince Edward Island. The Trout River meets the sea at Stanley Bridge, on the Island's north shore. More precisely, the pond, which was created by the damming of the creek in the early 1980s (a time when such riparian interference was not verboten), sits in a shallow valley just south of the Hazel Grove Road in Hazel Grove, PEI. This idyllic setting is where I grew up and where my mother and my brother's family still live. We would skate on the pond in winter and raft on it in summer. Many suppers were fished from its waters—quite effortlessly, since delaying suppertime for the trout was all it took to get them to rise to bait or a fly. I remember one time seeing a big beaver amble upstream, only to encounter the dam my father had built. Clearly intruding on some other beaver's territory, he turned around and headed back downstream.

**Cynthia Woodman Kerkham on "With No Sweet Water":** This is an ekphrastic poem written in response to a series of three large, wall-sized photographs of Xinkai river in northern China taken by the artist Li Xinmo. I spoke with Xinmo about the work, the river, and its industrial polluting. The body of a young woman was found in the river, and the artist photographed herself walking into Xinkai as a statement of connection between the violence done against the young woman and the river. We need to put our bodies on the line to stop the murderous poisoning of the waters and of the planet, the artist seems also to be saying. I was further inspired to collaborate with Chinese-speaking friends to translate the poem as a gesture towards the universality of our struggle for clean water and the need for cooperation across the man-made borders of nation states. Dirty water has no borders.

**David Yerex Williamson on "Warren's Landing":** Warren's Landing is a former fishing village, south of the Cree community of Norway House, Manitoba, accessible only by boat or snowmobile. From the early 20th Century until the 1970s, it was a central stop for passenger and commercial boats from Winnipeg to Norway House and was a processing site for the fishing industry. It was the original site of the Hudson Bay Company post that later moved to Norway House. Forty people lived in the community year-round, most without electricity or running water. The last residents moved to Norway House in 1986, including my wife's family. My father-in-law was a commercial fisher for over fifty years. The community remains a summer site for the fishing industry but the infrastructure and natural shoreline have deteriorated. In the 1970s, Manitoba Hydro developed an electrical generating dam on the Nelson River. To increase water flow to the dam, Manitoba Hydro carved two channels near Warren's Landing which affected shorelines and local economic and cultural traditions. I spent many afternoons with my father-in-law, learning about the changes in landscape and a lifestyle about which I knew very little. After my father-in-law passed, I wrote this poem.

**Joe Zucchiatti on "Parts Per Billion":** In the late 1940s, early 1950s, my grandfather and great grandfather built a rough-hewn cabin with no road access on Rainy Lake, just outside Fort Frances, Ontario, right next to a railroad track and a swamp. To a young boy visiting there in the summer, it was as idyllic as it gets. I visit there most every summer with my family, and the place still teems with swampy magic: the birds sing the same pretty songs as they did when I was a kid; the frog chorus at night; fireflies; garter snakes; leeches; mud turtles; cicadas—forget it. But it seems to me that there are fewer of these creatures than when I was a kid: getting a leech on your skin is a special occasion rather than a daily occurrence, and the fish are now so scarce, my family will even eat Northern Pike, which they'd previously scorned as a trash fish. My dad and uncles still drink the lightly filtered lake water, which is slightly yellow and tastes of swamp. They think I'm a wimp for drinking bottled water, but I don't like having diarrhea enough to volunteer for it.

# Acknowledgements

John Barton's "Palm Springs" was first published in *Hypothesis* by House of Anansi Press in 2001. Reprinted with the permission of John Barton. The book is now out of print.

"The Birds, Butterflies, and Snakes of Hamilton, Ontario" appeared in Gary Barwin's *No TV for Woodpeckers,* Wolsak & Wynn, 2018.

"Mountain Stream," by Lee Beavington was previously published in *Pathways: The Ontario Journal of Outdoor Education,* Summer 2017, 29(4), p. 36.

"Green Rain" by Terri Brandmueller was originally published in the now-defunct online poetry journal *Crested Myna Press,* 2007.

"Sounds a River Makes" by Claire Caldwell will also appear in her second full-length collection, *Gold Rush,* Invisible Publishing, April 2020.

Terry Ann Carter's haiku was inspired by "Working With Beavers to Restore Watersheds", Cathy Dowd, July 15, 2015, www.usda.gove/media/blog/2015/07/15/working-beavers-restore-watersheds.

"Stone's Deep Accord, its Steady Presence", by Wendy Donawa first appeared in *Thin Air of the Knowable,* Brick Books, 2017.

Alisa Gordaneer's poem "Flying River" is an erasure poem from an article in *The Atlantic* "Trees Could Change the Climate More Than Scientists Thought" by Gabriel Popkin and Quanta, Published October 13, 2018.

*TreeTalk: Winnipeg* by Ariel Gordon will be published as a limited-edition chapbook and trade poetry collection in fall 2020 with Winnipeg's At Bay Press.

"Under Western Water: Returning to Work" by Richard Harrison appears in *On Not Losing My Father's Ashes in the Flood* (Wolsak & Wynn, 2016), pages 60-62.

"Walk to the Wetlands" by Diana E. Hayes first appeared in *Labyrinth of Green,* © Plumleaf Press, Summer 2019.

"Lost Waterfalls" by Steven Heighton appeared in *Brick Magazine* and in *The Address Book,* House of Anansi, 2004.

"High Water Mark," by Maureen Hynes appears in, *Sotto Voce,* Brick Books, 2019.

"Water Crossings" by Elena Johnson appears in *The Enpipe Line: 70,000 km of poetry written in resistance to the Northern Gateway pipeline proposal,* ed. Jen Currin et al. Smithers, BC: Creekstone Press, 2012. Sources of found text for this poem are from the British Columbia Ministry of Forests, *The Ecology of the Sub-Boreal Spruce Zone,* 1998 and a website that is no longer available: Enbridge, Northern Gateway Pipeline website: *Project Info: FAQs,* 2011.

"Exorcise" by Elee Kraljii Gardiner was published in *PRISM International* 57.3 Ruin, Spring 2019.

"Bute Inlet" by Zoë Landale is from *Poetry Ireland Review,* Issue 99.

"Not the Lake" by Christine Lowther was first published in *The Malahat Review,* Spring 2017, Issue 198

"Kilrane" is included in Wendy McGrath's most recent poetry *A Revision of Forward,* NeWest Press, 2015.

"Homecoming" by David Martin was originally published in a chapbook published by Edmonton's Olive Reading Series titled *How Could You* (2019).

"The Water Heart" by Charlie Neyelle and Thos Nesbitt is the story of the Water Heart and is part of the traditional knowledge and culture of the Sahtugot'ine. The Elders of the Sahtugot'ine have kept and passed this story down through many generations. They revealed the story during the preparation of *The Water Heart: a Management plan for Great Bear Lake,* from 2002 to 2005. Charlie and Thos have merely put the story into the form of a poem, so as to share it with others.

"You Make Me Ache River..." by Catherine Owen will be published in her collection *Riven,* ECW Press, 2020.

"Falling Scene" by Jeremy Pataky borrows and adapts a line from Adam Zagajewski's poem "Try to Praise the Mutilated World".

"Fish Ladder" by John Pass is from *Water Stair*, Oolichan Books, 2000.

Kirsten Pendreigh's poem "Planetary Hubris" first appeared in *Prairie Fire Magazine* (Spring 2019 Issue. Vol. 40. No.1).

"Peace Country" by Pamela Porter appeared in *Defending Darkness*, published by Ronsdale Press, Vancouver, BC, 2016.

"I could simply give in" appears in D.C. Reid's book *These Elegies*, published in 2018 by Ekstasis Editions; it is part of a suite titled: A Brief Tour of Human Consciousness.

An earlier version of Harold Rhenisch's "The Promise of Rivers Shanty" appeared in Motherstone, by Country Lights Publishing, in 108 Mile Ranch, 2010.

"This Poem is One Pillar" by Kelly Shepherd appears in *Insomnia Bird: Edmonton Poems*, Thistledown Press, 2018.

"-40°C" by Eleonore Schönmaier appears in *Wavelengths of Your Song*, McGill Queen's University Press, 2013.

"A Brief History of Hamilton Mountain, from 1789" by John Terpstra, previously published in *Geez Magazine* (Spring 2019, Issue 52).

"When the Rain Comes" was published in Russell Thornton's *The Broken Face*, Harbour Publishing, 2018.

"Lost Stream" by Fiona Tinwei Lam appears in *Odes & Laments*, Caitlin Press, 2019.

"where" from *river woman* by Katherena Vermette (2018). Reproduced with permission from House of Anansi Press, Toronto. www.houseofanansi.com.

"The Pond" by Zachariah Wells is from *Track & Trace*, Biblioasis, 2009.

Excerpt from *beholden* reprinted by permission of the publisher from *beholden: a poem as long as the river*, © 2018 Rita Wong and Fred Wah, Talonbooks, Vancouver, B.C. 2018.

Derk Wynand's "Observation" previously appears in *Pointwise*, Fiddlehead Poetry Books, 1979.

## Yvonne Blomer's acknowledgements

I want to acknowledge the awesomeness of Publisher Vici Johnstone at Caitlin Press for being so utterly open to publishing not only this book but a trio of water-based anthologies following *Refugium: Poems for the Pacific*. Thanks also to Caitlin Press staff Sarah Corsie and Monica Miller. Huge thanks to artist Sharon Montgomery for the original art she's made for the book cover (check her out here: www.sharon-montgomery.net). Also big thanks to Barbara Pelman and Amy Reiswig for help in selecting the poems from the massive Yes/Maybe pile. I'm grateful to all the poets, those whose work I was able to include in the anthology, and all those who submitted work but were not included. I'm grateful for the written word, and the deep contemplation and care of poets who are also concerned with our waterways and watersheds. The sweet water I know best includes Thetis Lake, Beaver and Elk Lake, Fork Lake, Durance Lake, The Cowichan River, Lake Cowichan, Nanaimo River and other smaller waterways on Vancouver Island, though I swam and sailed on Skeleton Lake as a child. I am thankful for water, for we live on, from, and in it as do our trees, bees and futures. Thanks always to my husband Rupert Gadd and son Colwyn Blomer Gadd for mischief and love and for keeping me on solid earth. Thanks also to Frodo for the woods and watery paths.

The quote from Seamus Heaney on page 8 is from the poem "Anahorish" as it appears in *New Selected Poems 1966-1987*, Faber and Faber, 1990: London.

Quote from Katharine Norbury on page 8 is from the article "The top 10 books about rivers," *The Guardian*, February 18, 2015.

The quote on the water cycle on page 56 is from an article titled "The Fundamentals of the Water Cycle," from www.usgs.gov/special-topic/water-science-school/.

The Langston Hughes quote on page 60 is from the poem "The Negro Speaks of Rivers," as it appears on www.poets.org.

On the same page, Aimee Nezhukumatathil's quote is from "Naming the Heartbeats," in her collection *Oceanic*, Copper Canyon Press, 2018.

The quote from Mark Twain on page 118 is credited to Mark Twain, and others. Found on the internet.

The quote from *National Geographic* on page 118 is from "Fragile Life in Freshwater: Glimpses of the endangered world that lies below the surface of rivers, creeks and lakes" in *Proof, National Geographic*, October 2019, p 14.

The quote from William Stafford on page 118 is from his poem "Ask Me" as sent to me by the marvelous Barbara Pelman and found on www.poemhunter.com.

**I read and pondered the following during the editing of this book:**
The blog based on the UN Report on Sustainable Development from the IPBES at https://www.un.org/sustainabledevelopment/blog/2019/05/nature-decline-un-precedented-report/

Jan Zwicky and Robert Bringhurst's book *Learning to Die: Wisdom in the Age of Climate Crisis,* University of Regina Press, 2018.

Multiple articles and writings by Rita Wong.

And much more…thanks also to The Intercept and its piece "The Right to a Future – with Naomi Klein and Greta Thunberg," www.theintercept.com.

Thank you to Philip Kevin Paul.

**by the way:**
"Three-quarters of the land-based environment and about 66 percent of the marine environment have been significantly altered by human actions. On average these trends have been less severe or avoided in areas held or managed by Indigenous Peoples and Local Communities," from IPBES Global Assessment Report on Biodiversity and Ecosystem Services.